Curiosity

Evokes a sense of exploration and a complete guide for grade X - Physics

SHUBHAM SRIVASTAVA

B.Ed, M.Sc Physics,

M.A. Education

To you,

Dear learners,

for making this journey

worthwhile..

Contents

Acknowledgments...06

Introduction..07

Course Structure and Syllabus...09-11

List of Practicals..11-13

Question paper design...14

Chapter 1: Light – Reflection and Refraction...15-68

    NCERT in text questions with solutions.. 69-72

Chapter 2:Human eye and the colourful world...73-91

    NCERT in text questions with solutions...92

Chapter 3: Electricity..93-117

    NCERT in text questions with solutions...118-125

Chapter 4: Magnetic effect of current..127-143

    NCERT in text questions with solutions...144-146

Space for Notes..147-150

Acknowledgments

The creation of this book has been a collaborative effort, and i would like to express my sincere gratitude to the following:

Reviewers: I am indebted to the reviewers who generously donated their time and expertise to provide valuable feedback on the content and presentation of this book. Their insights and suggestions have been instrumental in shaping this book into a valuable resource for students.

My family and friends: I am grateful for the unwavering support and encouragement i received from my family and friends throughout this project. Special thanks to my wife *Shrishti* for the unconditional support which led to the timely completion of this book.

And you, the Student: Finally i acknowledge you for being the most essential part of this journey. Your curiosity, dedication and desire to learn Physics is what this book is all about. I hope this book ignites your passion for Science and empowers you to explore the wonders of this universe.

Introduction

Physics is the study of matter, energy and their interactions- it's the fundamental science that underpins our understanding of the universe around us.

This book is your guide in exploring this amazing world. You will delve into topics that would spark your curiosity and challenge you to think critically.

Learning physics is more than just memorizing facts and formulae. It's about developing a way of thinking that allows you analyse situations, solve problems and understand the world in a new and exciting way.

This book is filled with engaging explanations, clear illustrations and real world applications that will bring physics to life. We will explore everyday phenomenon and delve deeper into concepts that pique your interest.

So, buckle up and get ready for an incredible journey! As you turn the pages, remember: there are no bad questions in Physics, only a universe waiting to be explored.

Let's begin!

Course Structure for Annual Examination provided by CBSE

COURSE STRUCTURE

CLASS X

(Annual Examination)

Marks: 80

Unit No.	Unit	Marks
I	Chemical Substances-Nature and Behaviour	25
II	World of Living	25
III	Natural Phenomena	12
IV	Effects of Current	13
V	Natural Resources	05
	Total	80
	Internal assessment	20
	Grand Total	100

Theme: Materials

Unit I: Chemical Substances - Nature and Behaviour

Chemical reactions: Chemical equation, Balanced chemical equation, implications of a balanced chemical equation, types of chemical reactions: combination, decomposition, displacement, double displacement, precipitation, endothermic exothermic reactions, oxidation and reduction.

Acids, bases and salts: Their definitions in terms of furnishing of H+ and OH– ions, General properties, examples and uses, neutralization, concept of pH scale (Definition relating to logarithm not required), importance of pH in everyday life; preparation and uses of Sodium Hydroxide, Bleachingpowder, Baking soda, Washing soda and Plaster of Paris.

Metals and nonmetals: Properties of metals and non-metals; Reactivity series; Formation and properties of ionic compounds; Basic metallurgical processes; Corrosion and its prevention.

Carbon compounds: Covalent bonding in carbon compounds. Versatile nature of carbon. Homologous series. Nomenclature of carbon compounds containing functional groups (halogens, alcohol, ketones, aldehydes, alkanes and alkynes), difference between saturated hydro carbons and unsaturated hydrocarbons. Chemical properties of carbon compounds (combustion, oxidation, addition and substitution reaction). Ethanol and Ethanoic acid (only properties and uses), soaps and detergents.

Theme: The World of the Living

Unit II: World of Living

Life processes: 'Living Being'. Basic concept of nutrition, respiration, transport and excretion in plants and animals.

Control and co-ordination in animals and plants: Tropic movements in plants; Introduction of plant hormones; Control and co-ordination in animals: Nervous system; Voluntary, involuntary and reflex action; Chemical co-ordination: animal hormones.

Reproduction: Reproduction in animals and plants (asexual and sexual) reproductive health - need and methods of family planning. Safe sex vs HIV/AIDS. Child bearing and women's health.

Heredity and Evolution: Heredity; Mendel's contribution- Laws for inheritance of traits: Sex determination: brief introduction: (topics excluded - evolution; evolution and classification and evolution should not be equated with progress).

Theme: Natural Phenomena
Unit III: Natural Phenomena

Reflection of light by curved surfaces; Images formed by spherical mirrors, centre of curvature, principal axis, principal focus, focal length, mirror formula (Derivation not required),magnification. Refraction; Laws of refraction, refractive index.

Refraction of light by spherical lens; Image formed by spherical lenses; Lens formula (Derivation not required); Magnification. Power of a lens.
Functioning of a lens in human eye, defects of vision and their corrections, applications of spherical mirrors and lenses.

Refraction of light through a prism, dispersion of light, scattering of light, applications in dailylife (excluding colour of the sun at sunrise and sunset).

Theme: How Things Work

Unit IV: Effects of Current

Electric current, potential difference and electric current. Ohm's law; Resistance, Resistivity, Factors on which the resistance of a conductor depends. Series combination of resistors, parallel combination of resistors and its applications in daily life. Heating effect of electric current and its applications in daily life. Electric power, Interrelation between P, V, I and R.

Magnetic effects of current: Magnetic field, field lines, field due to a current carrying conductor, field due to current carrying coil or solenoid; Force on current carrying conductor, Fleming's Left Hand Rule, Direct current. Alternating current: frequency of AC. Advantage of AC over DC. Domestic electric circuits.

Theme: Natural Resources

Unit V: Natural Resources

Our environment: Eco-system, Environmental problems, Ozone depletion, waste production and their solutions. Biodegradable and non-biodegradable substances.

Note for the Teachers:

1. The chapter Management of Natural Resources (NCERT Chapter 16) will not be assessed in the year-end examination. However, learners may be assigned to read this chapter and encouraged to prepare a brief write up to any concept of this chapter in their Portfolio. This may be for Internal Assessment and credit may be given Periodic Assessment/Portfolio).

2. The NCERT text books present information in boxes across the book. These help students to get conceptual clarity. However, the information in these boxes would not be assessed in the year-end examination.

PRACTICALS

Practical should be conducted alongside the concepts taught in theory classes.

LIST OF EXPERIMENTS

1.   A. Finding the pH of the following samples by using pH paper/universal indicator: **Unit-I**
    (i)   Dilute Hydrochloric Acid
    (ii)   Dilute NaOH solution
    (iii)   Dilute Ethanoic Acid solution
    (iv)   Lemon juice
    (v)   Water
    (vi)   Dilute Hydrogen Carbonate solution

B. Studying the properties of acids and bases (HCl & NaOH) on the basis of their reaction with:

Unit-I

    a)   Litmus solution (Blue/Red)
    b)   Zinc metal
    c)   Solid sodium carbonate

2.   Performing and observing the following reactions and classifying them into: **Unit-I**

    A.   Combination reaction

    B.   Decomposition reaction

    C.   Displacement reaction

    D.   Double displacement reaction

        (i)   Action of water on quicklime

        (ii) Action of heat on ferrous sulphate crystals

        (iii) Iron nails kept in copper sulphate solution

        (iv) Reaction between sodium sulphate and barium chloride solutions

3.   Observing the action of Zn, Fe, Cu and Al metals on the following salt solutions: **Unit-I**

    i) $ZnSO_4(aq)$

    ii) $FeSO_4(aq)$

    iii) $CuSO_4(aq)$

    iv) $Al_2(SO_4)_3(aq)$

Arranging Zn, Fe, Cu and Al (metals) in the decreasing order of reactivity based on the above result.

4.   Studying the dependence of potential difference (V) across a resistor on the current (I) passing through it and determine its resistance. Also plotting a graph between V and I.   **Unit-IV**

5.   Determination of the equivalent resistance of two resistors when connected in series and parallel.   **Unit-IV**

6.   Preparing a temporary mount of a leaf peel to show stomata.   **Unit- II**

7.   Experimentally show that carbon dioxide is given out during respiration.   **Unit-II**

8.   Study of the following properties of acetic acid (ethanoic acid):   **Unit- I**

    i)   Odour

    ii) solubility in water

    iii) effect on litmus

    iv) reaction with Sodium Hydrogen Carbonate

9.   Study of the comparative cleaning capacity of a sample of soap in soft and hard water.   **Unit- I**

10.   Determination of the focal length of: **Unit-III**

i) Concave mirror

ii) Convex lens by obtaining the image of a distant object.

11. Tracing the path of a ray of light passing through a rectangular glass slab for different angles of incidence. Measure the angle of incidence, angle of refraction, angle of emergence and interpret the result. **Unit - III**

12. Studying (a) binary fission in *Amoeba*, and (b) budding in yeast and Hydra with the help of prepared slides. **Unit-II**

13. Tracing the path of the rays of light through a glass prism. **Unit-III**

14. Identification of the different parts of an embryo of a dicot seed (Pea, gram or red kidney bean).

Unit-II

PRESCRIBED BOOKS:
- Science-Textbook for class IX-NCERT Publication
- Science-Text book for class X- NCERT Publication
- Assessment of Practical Skills in Science-Class IX - CBSE Publication
- Assessment of Practical Skills in Science- Class X- CBSE Publication
- Laboratory Manual-Science-Class IX, NCERT Publication
- Laboratory Manual-Science-Class X, NCERT Publication
- Exemplar Problems Class IX – NCERT Publication
- Exemplar Problems Class X – NCERT Publication

Theory (80 marks) **Question Paper Design**

(Class X)

Subject: Science

Competencies	Total
Demonstrate Knowledge and Understanding	46 %
Application of Knowledge/Concepts	22 %
Formulate, Analyze, Evaluate and Create	32 %
	100%

Note:
- Typology of Questions: VSA including objective type questions, Assertion – Reasoning type questions; SA; LA; Source-based/ Case-based/ Passage-based/ Integrated assessment questions.
- An internal choice of approximately 33% would be provided.

Internal Assessment (20 Marks)
- **Periodic Assessment** - 05 marks + 05 marks
- **Subject Enrichment** (Practical Work) - 05 marks
- **Portfolio** - 05 marks

Suggestive verbs for various competencies
- **Demonstrate Knowledge and Understanding**
  - State, name, list, identify, define, suggest, describe, outline, summarize, etc.
- **Application of Knowledge/Concepts**
  - Calculate, illustrate, show, adapt, explain, distinguish, etc.
- **Formulate, Analyze, Evaluate and Create**
  - Interpret, analyze, compare, contrast, examine, evaluate, discuss, construct, etc.

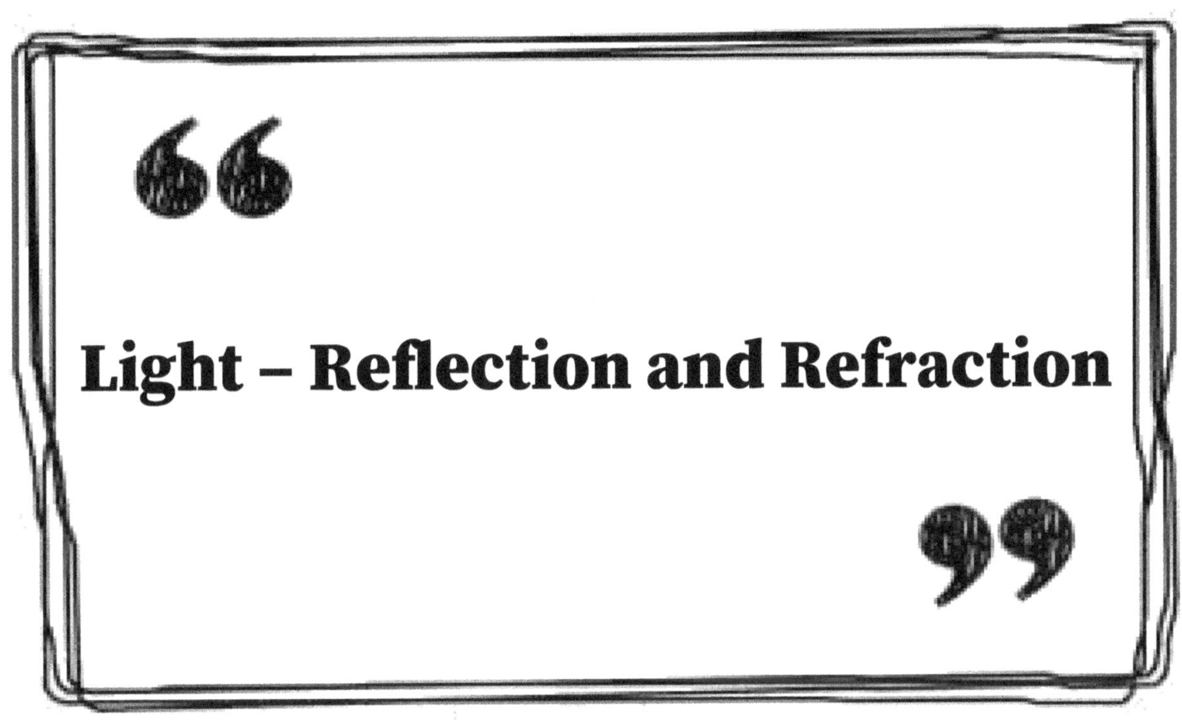

Light – Reflection and Refraction

Chapter 1: Light – Reflection and Refraction

What is Electromagnetic radiation?

Electromagnetic radiation consists of waves which travels through space carrying energy. They are made up of oscillating electric and magnetic fields. It includes Radio waves, Microwaves, Infrared, Light, Ultraviolet, X-rays and Gamma rays. The entire band is collectively called the Spectrum of Electromagnetic radiation.

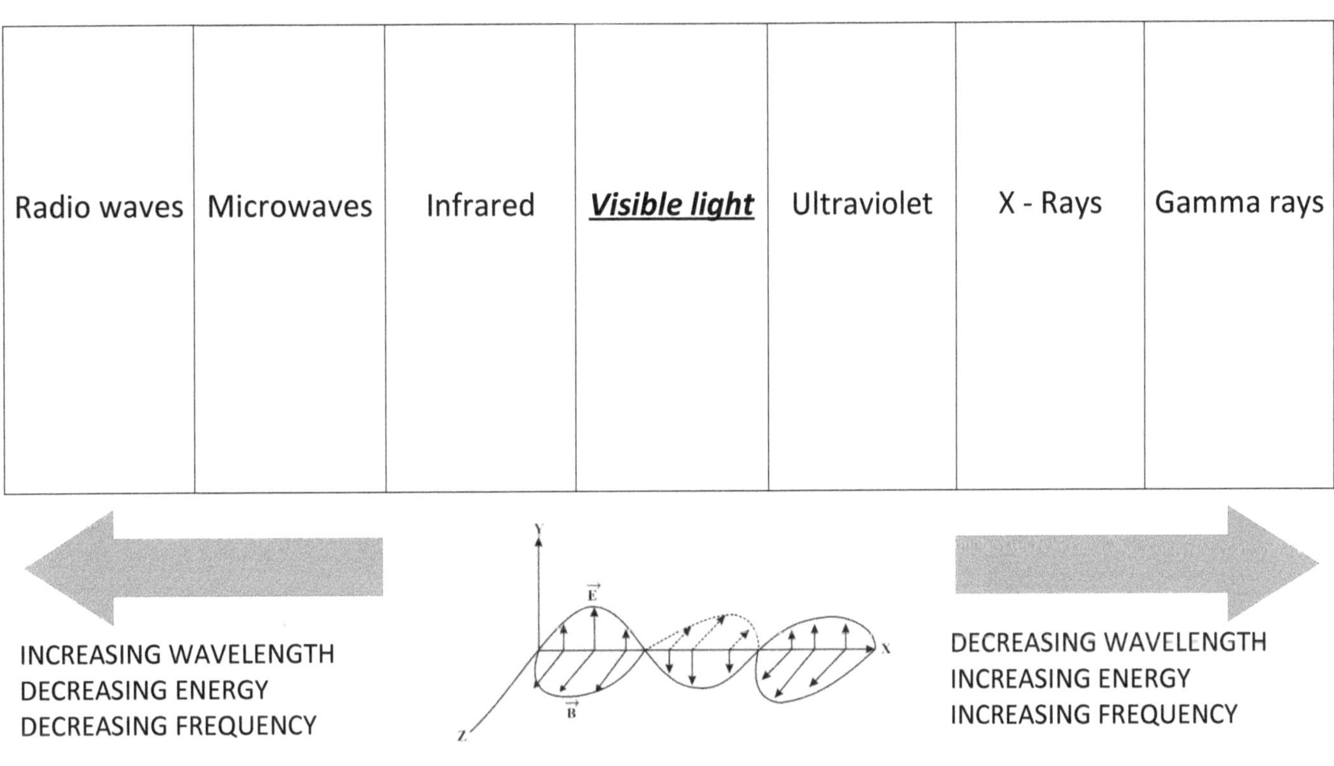

What is light?

Light is a form of electromagnetic radiation.

Light shows dual nature i.e. Sometimes it behaves as a ray and sometimes it behaves as a wave. If we consider it as a ray then we say that light is made of photons which can be understood as minute packets of energy. If we consider it as a wave then we say it is made up of oscillating electric and magnetic fields. So all we can say about light at this moment is that it behaves as a wave and as a particle, depending upon the circumstances. This concept is known as "wave-particle duality".

The details of dual nature of light will be taught in higher classes.

There are two major phenomenon of light which we will study in this chapter:

1. Reflection of light

2. Refraction of light

Reflection of light:

If a ray of light moving in a medium is incident on a surface in such a way that it bounces back into the same medium then the phenomenon is called Reflection of light. Light after striking an object reaches our eyes and this is how we are able to see things.

Now can you answer why we can not see see things in dark?

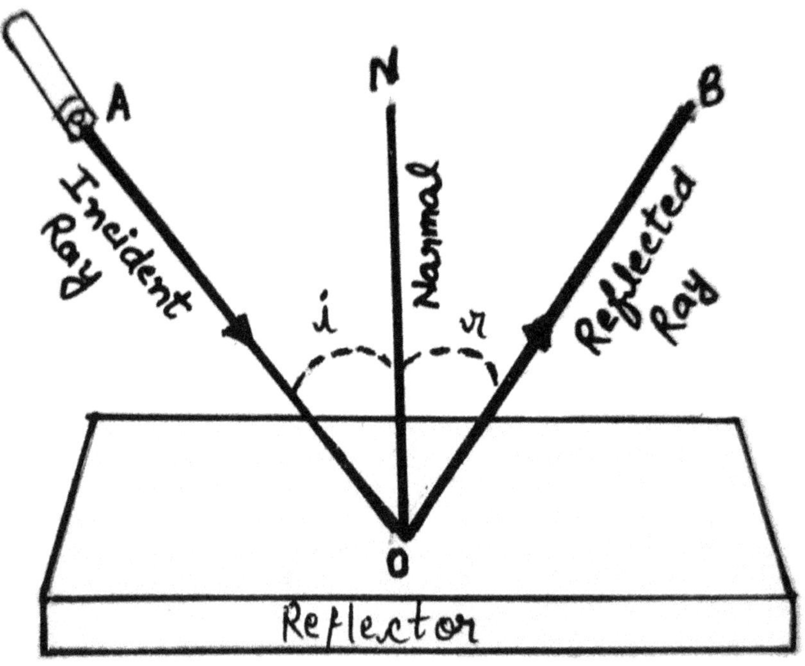

Terms associated with reflection of light:

1. Incident ray: Ray of light which strikes the object is known as Incident ray.

2. Reflected ray: Ray of light which bounces back after striking the object is known as Reflected ray.

3. Normal: An imaginary ray drawn perpendicular to the surface.

4. Angle of Incidence: Angle between the incident ray and the normal.

5. Angle of Reflection: Angle between the reflected ray and the normal.

6. Angle of Glance: Angle between the incident ray and the surface.

Laws of Reflection of light

There are two laws of reflection which are as follows:

1. The angle of incidence is equal to the angle of reflection.

2. The Incident ray, Reflected ray and the Normal at the point of incidence all lie in the same plane.

Note: The above mentioned laws of reflection are applicable to all type of reflecting surfaces whether they are plane or spherical.

Mirror

A mirror is an optical device which can reflect light. It's one side is used as a reflecting surface and the other side is a well polished surface.

Note: *One side of the mirror is always polished so that light can reflect back instead of passing away from it.*

Mirrors are of two types:

1. Plane mirror

2. Spherical mirror

Spherical Mirrors

The spherical mirrors can be used to converge or diverge the incoming rays. On the basis of their nature they are further classified into two types.

Concave spherical mirror: Such type of mirrors have to capability to converge the rays and are also called Converging mirrors. It's reflecting surface is curved inwards and the other surface is polished.

Convex spherical mirror: Such type of mirrors have to capability to diverge the rays and are also called Diverging mirrors. It's reflecting surface is curved outwards and the other surface is polished.

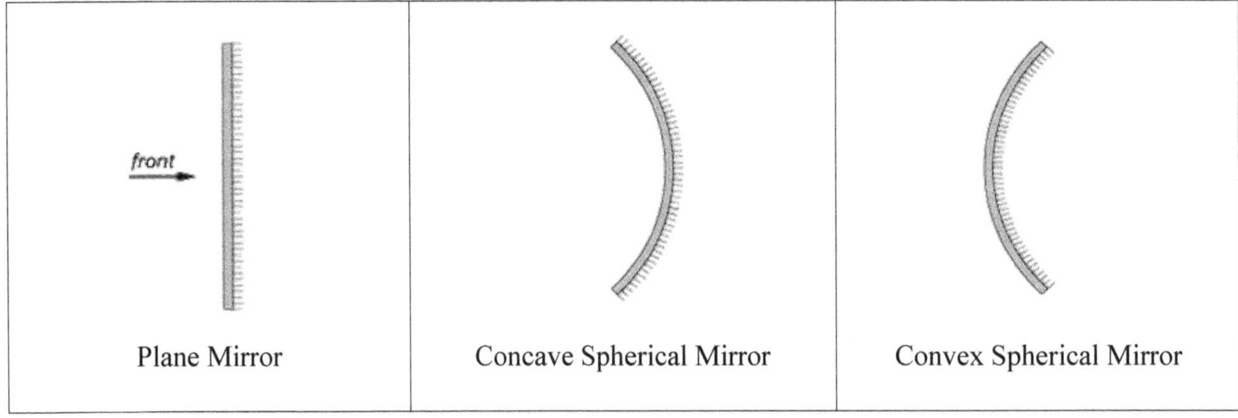

| Plane Mirror | Concave Spherical Mirror | Convex Spherical Mirror |

There are two types of images formed by mirrors:

1. Real Image

2. Virtual Image

Note: Images are named on the basis of type of Intersection of rays.

What is a Real Image?

The type of image formed by "actual intersection" of rays is called Real image. Since the intersection of rays is actual that is why it can be obtained on a screen. It should be remembered that a real image is always INVERTED in nature.

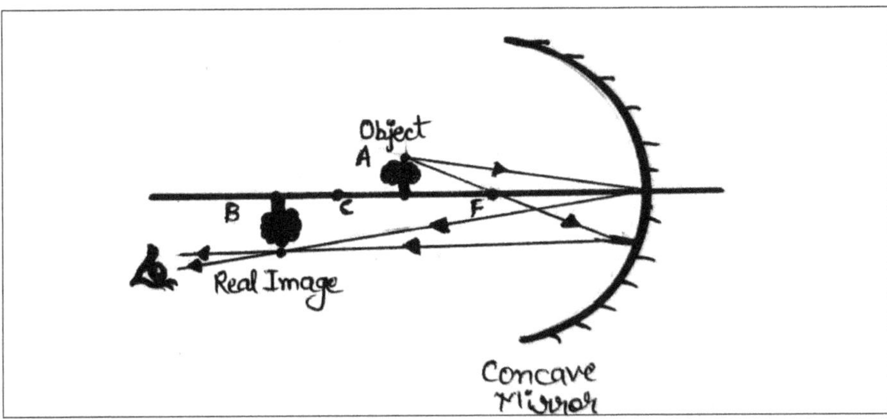

What is a Virtual image?

The type of image formed by "virtual intersection" of rays is called Virtual image. This type of image is formed when the rays do not actually intersect but instead *appear* to intersect at a point. Such type of image is erect and cannot be obtained on a screen.

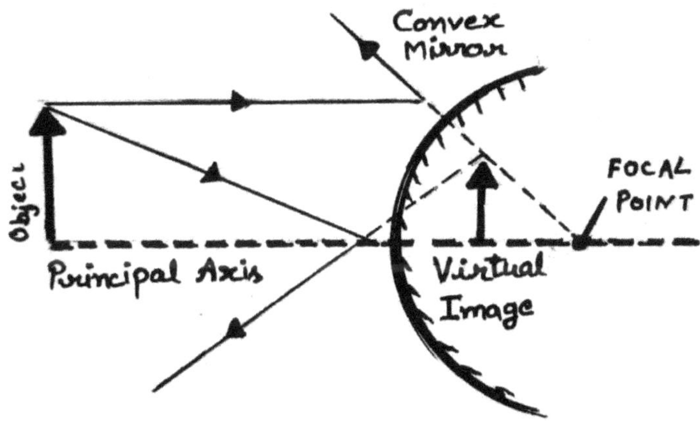

What is the difference between a real and a virtual image?

Real Image	Virtual Image
It is formed by actual intersection of rays.	It is formed when rays *appear* to intersect at a point.
It is inverted in nature.	It is erect in nature.
It can be obtained on a screen.	It can not be obtained on a screen.

What are ray diagrams?

With respect to a mirror, an object can be at different locations. With the help of ray diagrams we try to find out the position of the image with respect to the varying position of the object.

Laws to be followed for making ray diagrams:

a. If a ray of light passes parallel to the principal axis then after striking the mirror it will either pass through the principal focus or it appears to pass through the principal focus.

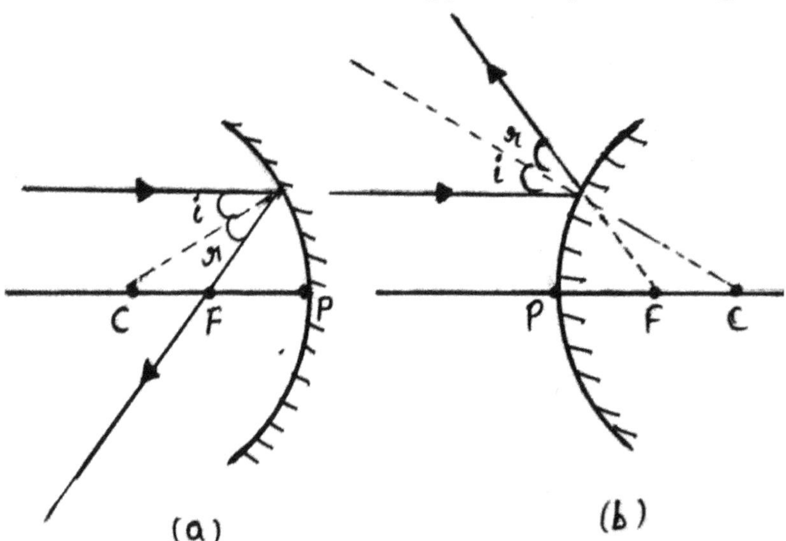

b. If a ray of light passes from the focus or if a ray of light is directed towards the focus then after striking the mirror it will pass parallel to the principal axis.

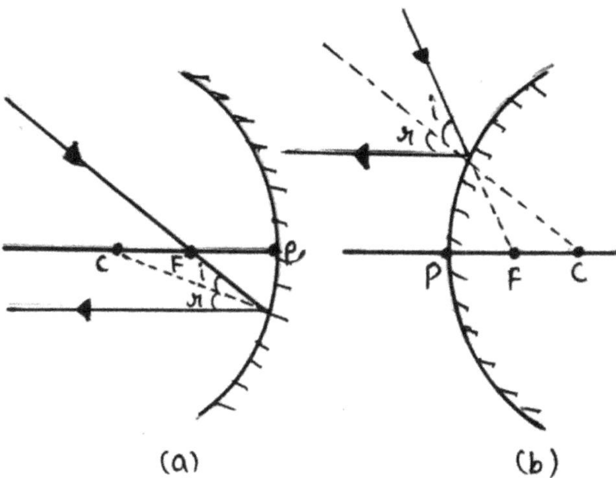

c. If a ray of light passes from the centre of curvature or is directed in the direction of centre of curvature and then strikes the mirror then after striking the mirror it will rebound on its original path.

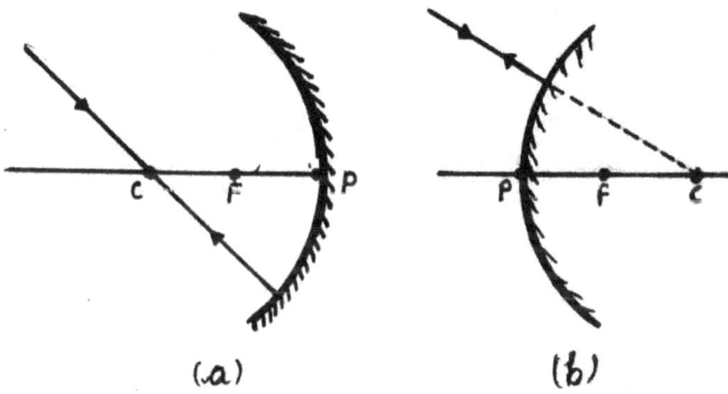

d. If a ray of light strikes the mirror obliquely at the pole then it will reflect in such a way that the angle of incidence is equal to the angle of reflection.

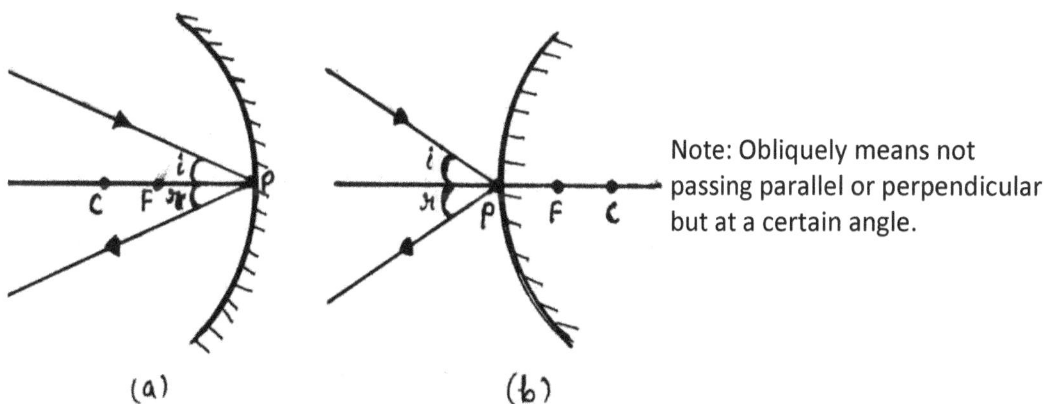

Note: Obliquely means not passing parallel or perpendicular but at a certain angle.

Ray diagrams of concave mirror:

Case 1: When the object is present at infinity.

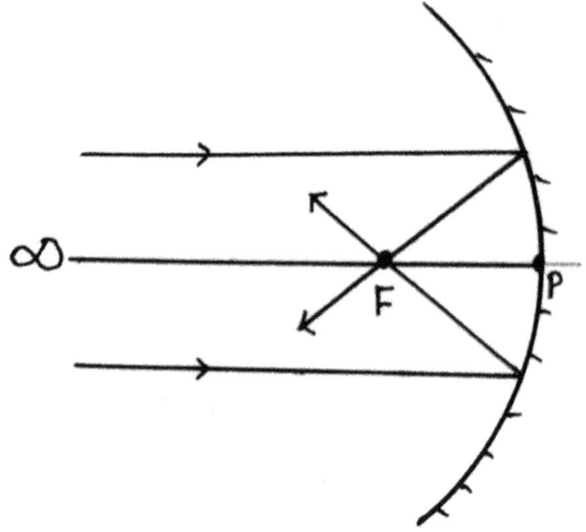

Properties of the image formed:

a. Image formed will be real.

b. Image formed will be inverted.

c. Image formed will be highly diminished.

d. Image will be formed at the principal focus.

Case 2: When the object is present beyond centre of curvature.

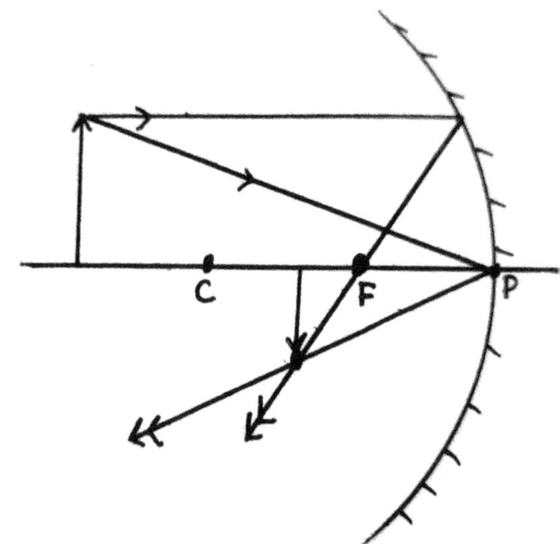

Properties of the image formed:

a. Image formed will be real.

b. Image formed will be inverted.

c. Image formed will be diminished.

d. Image will be formed between focus and the centre of curvature.

Case 3: When the object is present at the centre of curvature.

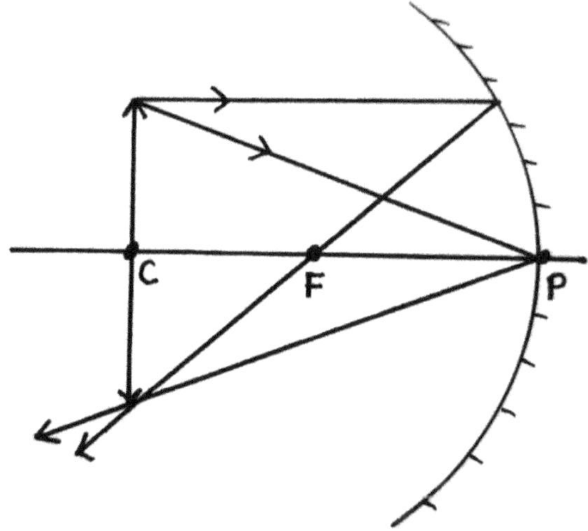

Properties of the image formed:

a. Image formed will be real.

b. Image formed will be inverted.

c. Image formed will be of the same size as that of the object.

d. Image will be formed at the centre of curvature.

Case 4: When the object is between centre of curvature and the focus.

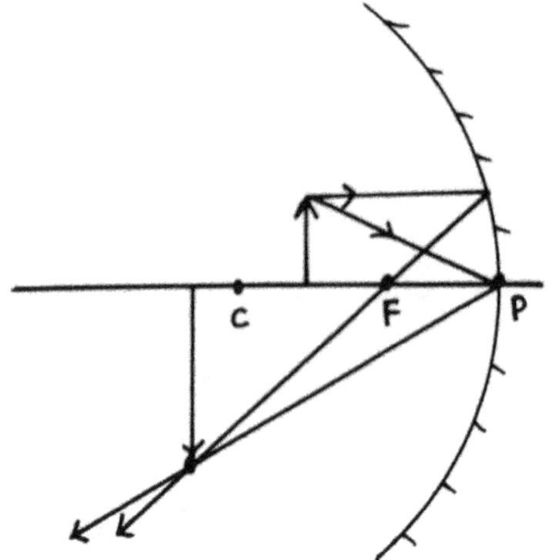

Properties of the image formed:

a. Image formed will be real.

b. Image formed will be inverted.

c. Image formed will be magnified.

d. Image will be formed beyond centre of curvature.

Case 5: When the object is at focus

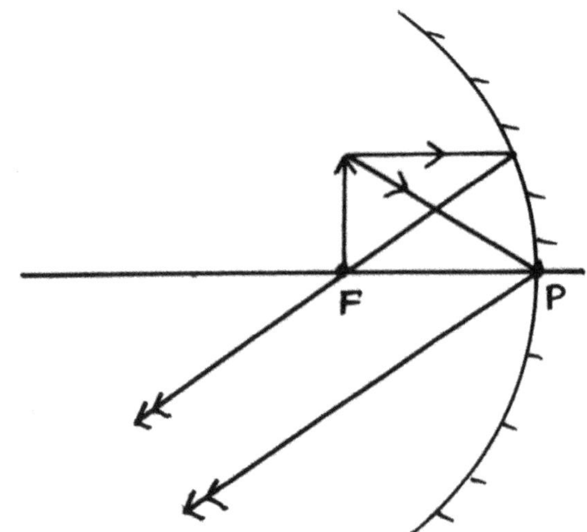

Properties of the image formed:

a. Image formed will be real.

b. Image formed will be inverted.

c. Image formed will be highly magnified.

d. Image will be formed at infinity.

Case 6: When the object is between focus and pole (Exceptional case)

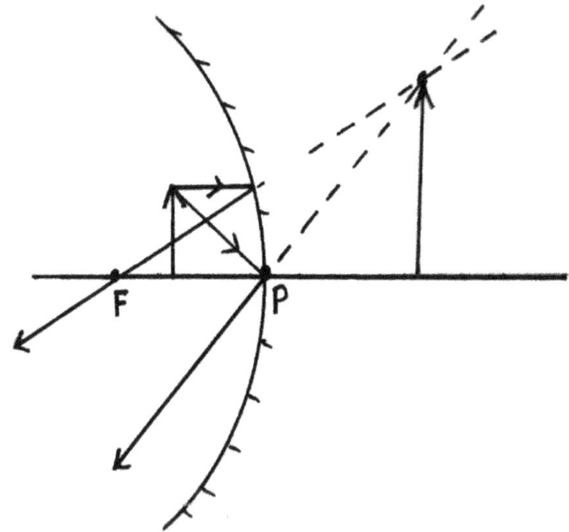

Properties of the image formed:

a. Image formed will be virtual.

b. Image formed will be erect.

c. Image formed will be magnified.

d. Image will be formed behind the mirror.

Note: *This is an exceptional case because this is the only case in concave mirror in which a virtual and erect image is formed.*

Trick to remember ray diagram of concave mirror:

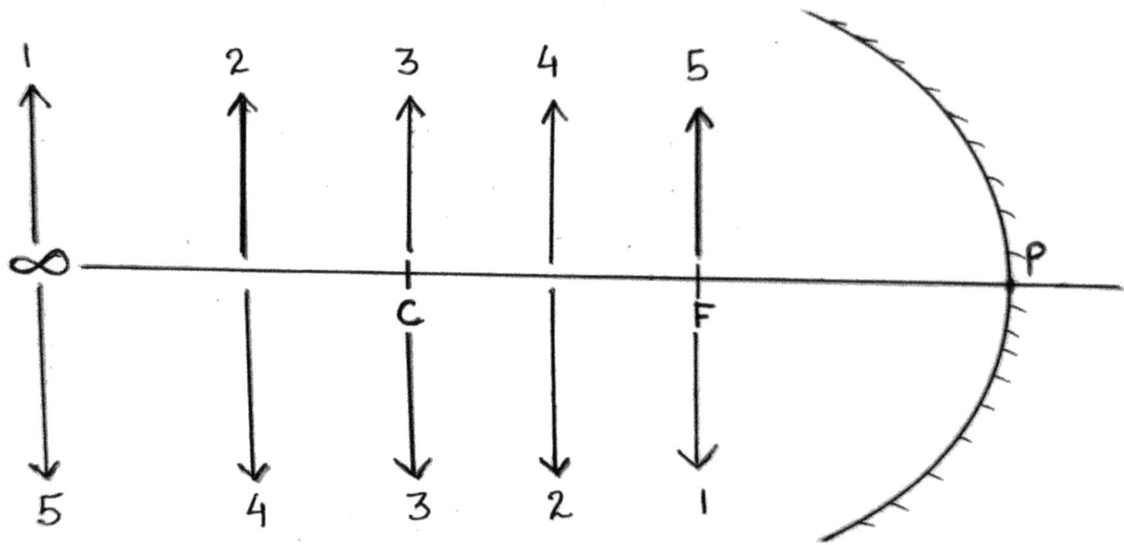

If you look at the diagram carefully you will notice that the numbers 1 – 5 above the principal axis represents the different position of the object.

The numbers 1 – 5 below the principal axis represents the different positions of the image.

All you need to remember is that same numbers above and below the principal axis represents the respective position of the object and the image.

For example: Junction 2 above the axis matches with junction 2 below the axis. This shows that if the object is at junction 2 then its image will be at junction 2 below the axis. Here junction 2 above the axis represents the position of the object beyond centre of curvature and the junction 2 below the axis represents the position of the image between focus and centre of curvature. That means if the object is beyond centre of curvature then its image will be formed between focus and centre of curvature.

In this way you can remember the relative positions of object and image before making the ray diagrams. The exceptional case is not a part of this trick.

Question: *Can you guess where will the image be formed if an object is positioned between focus and centre of curvature in front of a concave spherical mirror?*

If you can answer this question without drawing the ray diagram then you have understood the trick.

Ray diagrams of convex mirror:

Case 1: When the object is at infinity.

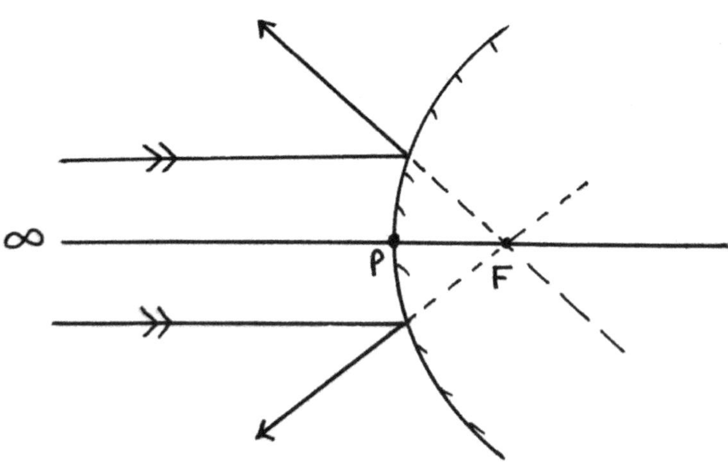

Properties of the image formed:

a. Image formed will be virtual.

b. Image formed will be erect.

c. Image formed will be highly diminished.

d. Image appears to form behind the mirror at the principal focus.

Case 2: When the object is at a finite distance.

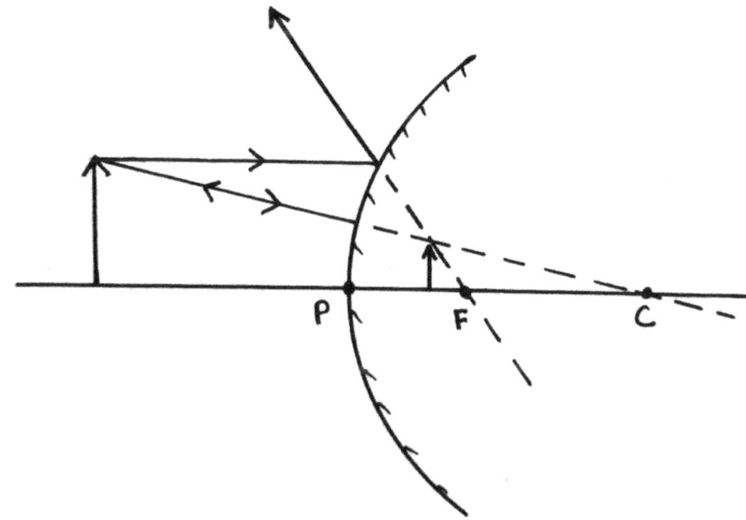

Properties of the image formed:

a. Image formed will be virtual.

b. Image formed will be erect.

c. Image formed will be diminished in nature.

d. Image appears to form behind the mirror between focus and pole.

Plane Mirror

A Plane Mirror has a flat reflective surface for light to strike and is polished from the other side. A plane mirror has infinite focal length. This is due to the fact that when parallel rays of light strike the plane mirror then the reflected rays are also parallel and parallel rays appears to meet at infinity.

Properties of image formed by a Plane mirror:

- A plane mirror always forms a virtual image.

- The image formed by a plane mirror is of the same size as that of the object.

- The image formed by a plane mirror appears to form behind the mirror such that the distance between the object and the mirror is equal to the distance between the mirror and the image.

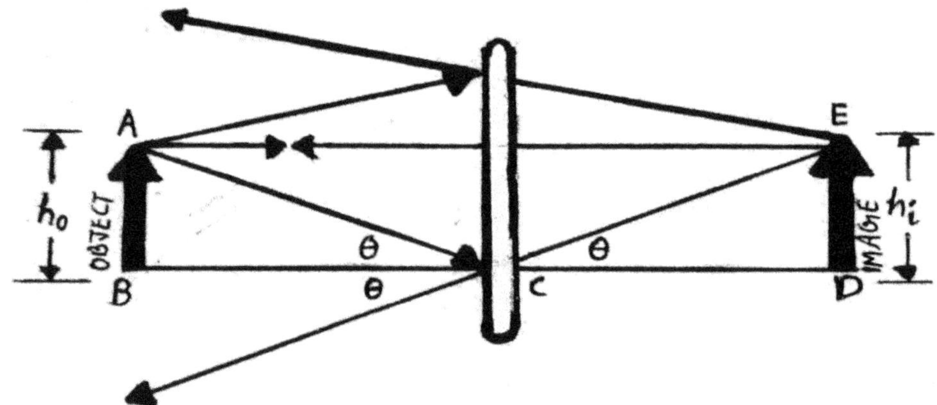

Important points regarding image formed by mirrors:

◆ In case of a concave spherical mirror there are six cases for image formation.

◆ In case of a convex spherical mirror there are only two cases for image formation.

◆ Concave spherical mirror is the only mirror which can produce real image as well as virtual image.

◆ Convex spherical mirror and Plane mirror can only produce virtual mirror.

◆ Concave spherical mirror can produce image of all sizes.

◆ Convex spherical mirror can only produce image smaller than the size of the object.

◆ Plane mirror can only produce image of the same size as that of the object.

Question: Which type of mirror always produce a real image?

Answer: There is no such mirror which always forms a real image. If you are thinking that the answer should be concave spherical mirror then read the question again and find out the word which contradicts your answer.

Question: Which type of mirror always produce a virtual image?

Answer: Convex spherical mirror and Plane mirror always produce a virtual image. Please note that mentioning only one of the above two mirrors would be insufficient to answer the above question.

Sign convention for Spherical mirrors:

While doing the calculations related to the spherical mirrors we shall follow the Cartesian Sign convention system. Here are the key points:

a. The pole of the mirror is supposed to be the origin.

b. The principal axis is supposed to be the x – axis.

c. The object shall always be kept to the left of the mirror and light from the object must fall on the mirror from the left side only.

d. All the measurements to the right of the pole are taken as positive and all the measurements to the left of the pole are taken as negative.

e. All the measurements above the principal axis are taken as positive and all the measurements below the principal axis are taken negative.

Note: Since the focal length of the concave spherical mirror is taken on the left side of the pole we will assume its value to be negative and since the focal length of the convex spherical mirror is taken on the right side of the pole we will assume its value to be positive.

Focal length of concave spherical mirror = negative

Focal length of convex spherical mirror = positive

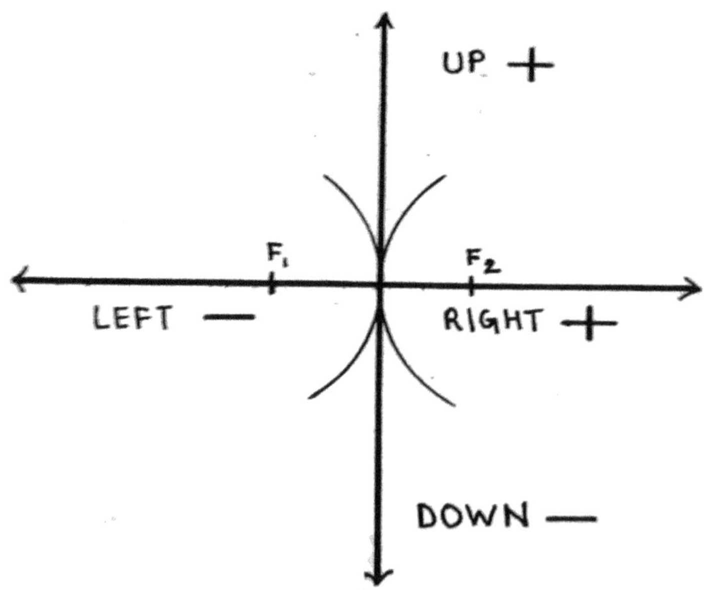

Mirror Formula

In case of a spherical mirror,

u = distance of the object from the mirror

v = distance of the image from the mirror

f = focal length

and thus the mirror formula is:

$$\frac{1}{f} = \frac{1}{v} + \frac{1}{u}$$

Magnification:

Magnification of the image can be defined as the ratio of height of the image to height of the object. In simple words magnification is that property of image which tells about the size of the image with respect to the object. The formula to calculate magnification is:

$$m = \frac{height\ of\ the\ image}{height\ of\ the\ object}$$

There is one more formula of magnification which is :

$$m = \frac{-v}{u}$$

Note: The values placed in the magnification and mirror formula must be placed "**along with the signs**" as per the sign convention.

Example:

Case 1: A concave spherical mirror of focal length 10 cm is used to form an image. The object is placed at a distance of 20 cm and the image is formed at 20 cm. Calculate magnification.

Case 2: A convex spherical mirror of focal length 10 cm is used to form an image. The object is placed at a distance of 20 cm and the image appears to form at a distance of 6.67 cm behind the mirror. Calculate magnification.

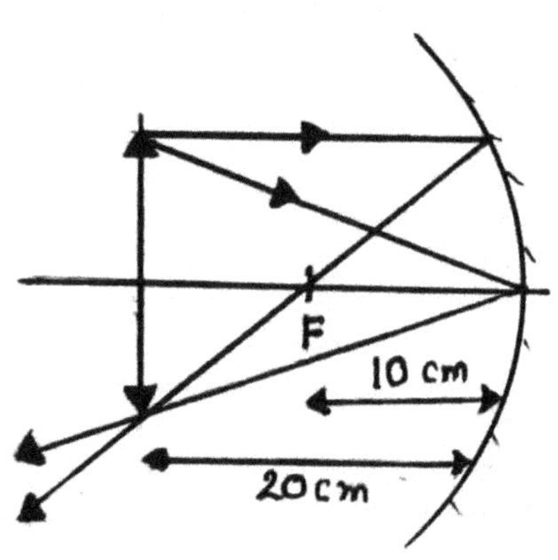

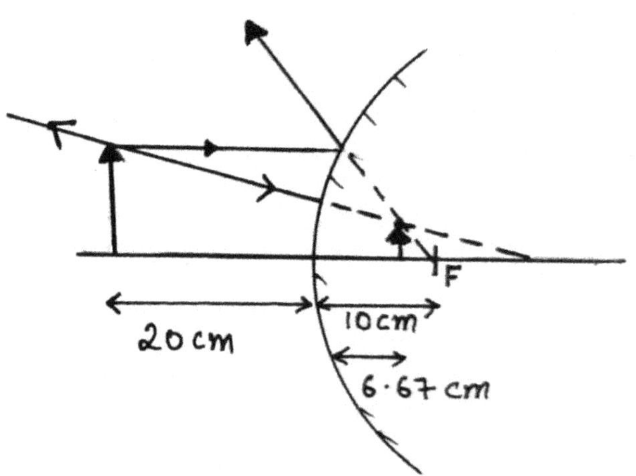

Case 1: Concave spherical mirror

$f = -10$ cm

$u = -20$ cm

$v = -20$ cm

$m = -(-20/-20) = -1$

Case 2: Convex spherical mirror

$f = 10$ cm

$u = -20$ cm

$v = 6.67$ cm

$m = -(6.67/-20) = 0.33$

Examples:

1. In case of a converging mirror of focal length 10cm an object is placed at a distance of 25cm. Find out the position of image with respect to the mirror. Also find out the magnification of the image.

Solution:

Since it's a converging mirror (concave mirror) therefore as per the sign convention negative sign will be used with focal length.

F = -10cm

u = -25cm

v = ?

using mirror formula:

$$\frac{1}{f} = \frac{1}{v} + \frac{1}{u}$$

Let's substitute the values now:

$$\frac{1}{-10} = \frac{1}{v} + \frac{1}{-25}$$

$$-\frac{1}{10} = \frac{1}{v} - \frac{1}{25}$$

$$-\frac{1}{10} + \frac{1}{25} = \frac{1}{v}$$

$$\frac{-5+2}{50} = \frac{1}{v} \qquad \text{(the L.C.M. of 25 and 10 is 50)}$$

$$\frac{-3}{50} = \frac{1}{v}$$

$$v = \frac{-50}{3} \text{cm}$$

Now let's calculate magnification

$$m = \frac{-v}{u}$$

$$m = -\frac{-50/3}{-25}$$

(note that the formula consists a minus sign and the values have their own sign)

$$m = -\frac{50}{3 \, x \, 25}$$

Note that in the above step, the minus sign in the numerator and denominator cancels each other but the minus sign of the formula is still left

$$m = -\frac{2}{3}$$

◆ This value of the magnification indicates that the size of the image is two-third of the size of the object. The minus sign in the magnification means that the image is real and inverted in nature.

2. In case of a convex mirror of focal length 15cm an object is placed at a distance of 30cm. Find out the position of image with respect to the mirror. Also find out the magnification of the image.

Solution:

Since it's a convex mirror therefore as per the sign convention positive sign will be used with focal length.

F = +15cm

u = -30cm

v = ?

using mirror formula:

$$\frac{1}{f} = \frac{1}{v} + \frac{1}{u}$$

$$\frac{1}{15} = \frac{1}{v} + \frac{1}{-30}$$

$$\frac{1}{15} = \frac{1}{v} - \frac{1}{30}$$

$$\frac{1}{15} + \frac{1}{30} = \frac{1}{v} \quad \text{(the L.C.M. of 15 and 30 is 30)}$$

$$\frac{2+1}{30} = \frac{1}{v}$$

$$\frac{3}{30} = \frac{1}{v}$$

$$\frac{1}{10} = \frac{1}{v}$$

v = 10 cm

(The positive value of v indicates the image will be formed on the right side i.e. behind the mirror)

Now let's calculate the value of magnification

$$m = \frac{-v}{u}$$

$m = -\dfrac{10}{-30}$ (note that the formula consists of a minus sign and the values have their own sign)

$$m = \frac{1}{3}$$

◆ The value of magnification shows that the image will be one-third the size of the object. Since the magnification is positive, it shows that the image is virtual and erect.

What does different values of magnification indicate?

a. If there is a minus sign in magnification then it indicates that the image is real and inverted in nature. For example if magnification is -3 then the image is real and inverted.

b. If the magnification is having a positive value then it indicates that the image is virtual and erect in nature. For example if magnification is 3 then the image is virtual and erect.

c. If the value of magnification is less than 1 (irrespective of the sign) then it indicates that the image is smaller than the object. For example if magnification is $-\frac{1}{3}$ then it indicates image is 3 times smaller than the object. At the same time we can see that there is minus sign which indicates real and virtual.

d. If the value of magnification is greater than 1 (irrespective of the sign) then it indicates that the image is bigger than the object. For example if magnification is -2.5 then it indicates image is 2.5 times bigger than the object. At the same time minus sign indicates that the image is real and virtual.

Practice question: If the magnification of an image is $\frac{4}{3}$ then state the properties of the image formed. Also state the type of mirror used.

Answer: Since the magnification is in positive then it indicates that the image is virtual and erect. Also the value of magnification is greater than one so it indicates that the image is bigger than the object.

Overall properties of the image:

a. Virtual

b. Erect

c. Magnified

d. It is formed by *__concave mirror__* since it is the only mirror which can produce a virtual magnified mirror.

Uses of Spherical mirrors:

1. Concave Spherical mirrors

i. They are used in torches.

ii. They are used in search lights.

iii. They are used in the headlights of vehicles.

iv. They are used as shaving mirrors.

v. They are used by dentists to see large images of the teeth.

vi. They are used in solar furnaces to concentrate sunlight to produce heat.

2. Convex Spherical mirrors

i. They are used as rear view mirrors in vehicles.

ii. They are used as side view mirrors in vehicles as it gives a wider field of view.

iii. It is used as a reflector in street light.

iv. It is used in ATM's to show the back side area of the person using the machine.

Note: It is always written on side view mirrors of the vehicles that *Objects in the mirror are closer than they appear.* If we look at the image formed by the convex spherical mirrors then we can notice that such type of mirrors always forms image which appears to form behind the mirror which technically increases the distance between object and image. This becomes the reason why objects in the convex spherical mirrors are closer than they appear.

Guess the answer: A mirror is fitted in a wall of Agra Fort to observe the full image of Taj Mahal. Can you guess the type of image used?

Use this space to right the answer: _______________________________

Reason: ____

Refraction of light:

When a ray of light travels from one transparent medium to another then there is some change in the path of light due to the bending of the ray of light. This phenomenon is called *Refraction of light.*

Cause of refraction of light:

Light travels with different speed in different medium. When there is a change in the medium then there is change in the speed of light and we say that the light is getting refracted.

Some applications of Refraction of light:

a. The bottom of a glass containing water appears to be raised due to refraction of light.

b. A pencil whose some portion is dipped in a glass of water appears to be bent due to refraction of light.

c. A lemon kept in a glass of water appears to be bigger in size due to refraction of light.

But what makes the light travels in different medium with different speed?

It is the **"Optical Density"** of every medium which makes the light travel with different speed in different medium. Please note that the optical density is different from mass density. *Optical density is the ability of a material to pass light through it.*

If the optical density of a medium is more than the other medium then the former medium is denser and the latter is rarer.

Suppose a ray of light passes from a rarer to a denser medium. In this case the speed of light will decrease. As opposite to the previous case if a ray of light passes from a denser to a rarer medium then the speed of light will increase.

Keypoints:

- The medium whose optical density is more is denser and the medium with less optical density is rarer.

- In a denser medium speed of light decreases and in a rarer medium speed of light increases.

- When a ray of light moves from one medium to another it's speed and wavelength changes but the frequency remains unaffected. Frequency changes only when there is change in source.

Now let's understand the shifting pattern of ray of light when it changes medium:

- When a ray of light passes from rarer to denser medium then it shifts towards the normal.

- When a ray of light passes from denser to rare medium then it shifts away from the normal.

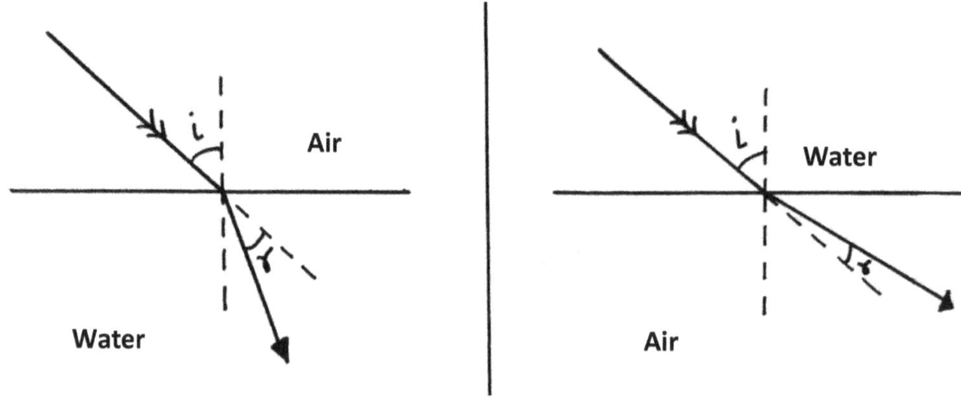

Laws of Refraction

a. The incident ray, refracted ray and the normal at the point of incidence all lie on the same plane.

b. The ratio of sine of angle of incidence to the sine of angle of refraction is a constant for a given pair of media. This law is also known as Snell's law.

Note that Snell's law is applicable when angle of incidence is between 0^0 to 90^0.

$$\frac{\sin i}{\sin r} = \text{constant (n)}$$

The above constant (n) is termed as Refractive Index. It is a unit less quantity since it is a ratio of same quantity.

Refractive Index

It is the Refractive Index which indicates the extent to which a ray of light will bent when it will pass from one medium to another.

Note: If a ray of light travels from one medium to another and the refractive index of first medium is lesser than the refractive index of second medium then the second medium is denser than the first medium. So we can say if the refractive index increases the medium becomes denser.

If $n_1 = 1.46$ and $n_2 = 1.54$ then the first medium will be rarer and the second medium will be denser.

Also when we compare the refractive index of two medium then we say that *speed of light will be more in the medium whose refractive index is less.*

Question: You are provided with refractive indexes of three mediums:

n_1= 1.42, n_2= 1.56 and n_3= 1.25.

In which medium will the speed of light be maximum?

Answer: The speed of light will be maximum in the third medium since it's refractive index is minimum.

- If a ray of light travels specifically from air to another medium then the refractive index of that medium can be calculated with the help of the below formula:

$$n = \frac{c}{v}$$ where c= speed of light in air/vacuum and v= speed of light in that medium

- Now it is not necessary that the ray of light will always travel from air to another medium so we have another formula to calculate the refractive index:

$$n = \frac{u}{v}$$ where u= velocity in the first medium and v = velocity in the second medium.

So over all we have three formulae for calculating the refractive index which are as follows:

$$n = \frac{\sin i}{\sin r}, \quad n = \frac{c}{v} \text{ and } n = \frac{u}{v}$$

The first formula will be used when you are provided with angles, the second formula will be used when ray of light travels from air to another medium and the third formula will be used when ray of light travels from any medium 1 to any medium 2.

Also note that by using the above mentioned formulae we get the refractive index of the second medium.

Question: The refractive index of water is 1.33. What do you understand from the statement?

Answer: The above statement means that the speed of light in water is 1.33 times slower that that in air.

Example: If a ray of light travels from air to a medium X then calculate the refractive index of the medium X with respect to air if the speed of light in air is 3 x 10^8 m/s and the speed of light in medium X is 2 x 10^8 m/s

Solution:

Here: c = 3 x 10^8 m/s

v = 2 x 10^8 m/s

so using the formula: $_a n_x = \dfrac{c}{v}$

$$_a n_x = \dfrac{3 \times 10^8}{2 \times 10^8}$$

$_a n_x = 1.5$

Here $_a n_x$ indicates refractive index of medium X with respect to air.

Example: If refractive index of medium 1 with respect to medium 2 is $\frac{4}{3}$ then what will be the refractive index of medium 2 with respect to medium 1?

Solution: In order to solve such type of questions we only need to find the reciprocal of refractive index provided.

$_2n_1$ = refractive index of medium 1 with respect to medium 2

$_1n_2$ = refractive index of medium 2 with respect to medium 1

so, if $_2n_1 = \frac{4}{3}$ then $_1n_2 = \frac{3}{4}$

Example: If the refractive index of glass with respect to air is 1.52 and refractive index of water with respect to air is 1.33 then calculate the refractive index of glass with respect to water.

Solution: In such questions where two refractive indexes are given we use the below formula:

Here: $n_{glass} = 1.52$ and $n_{water} = 1.33$ so,

$$_{water}n_{glass} = \frac{n_{glass}}{n_{water}}$$

$$_{water}n_{glass} = \frac{1.52}{1.33}$$

$$_{water}n_{glass} = 1.14$$

Types of refractive index:

a. *Absolute refractive index*: It is the refractive index of a medium with respect to air.

b. *Relative refractive index:* It is the refractive index of a medium with respect to a specific medium.

The absolute refractive index of water is 1.33 which means that the refractive index of water with respect to air is 1.33.

The refractive index of glass with respect to air is 1.52 but the refractive index of glass with respect to water is 1.14 so we can see that the relative refractive index of a medium keeps changing. It depends on the medium with respect to which we are calculating it.

Question: Is it possible that a ray of light travels from one medium to another but still there is no change in the path of light?

Answer: Yes, it is possible! If the Refractive index of both the mediums are very close to each other then the ray of light moves from one medium to another without any deflection. In fact if we talk about the ground reality then there is actually slight change in the path of light but that change is very small so we neglect it and say that there is no change in the path of light. Also, if the angle of incidence is 0^0 then in this case also there is no change in the path of light. Again just to make it clear, there would be some minute change in the path of light in this case also but since that change is too small so we neglect it and say that there is no change in the path of light.

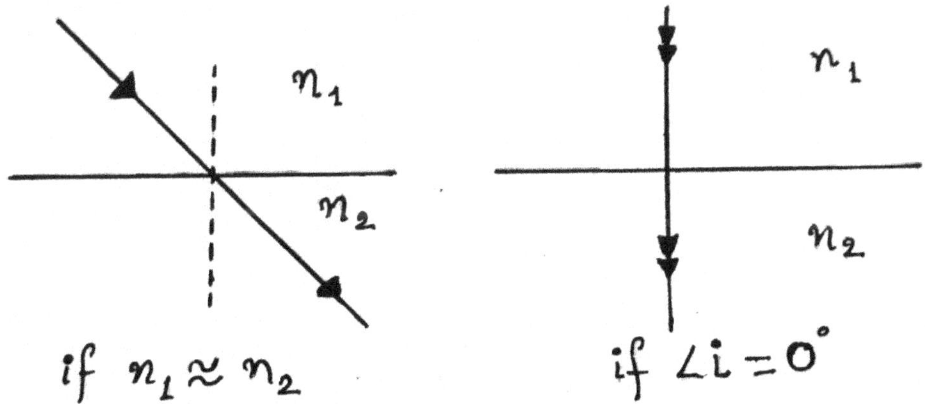

Refraction of light through a rectangular glass slab

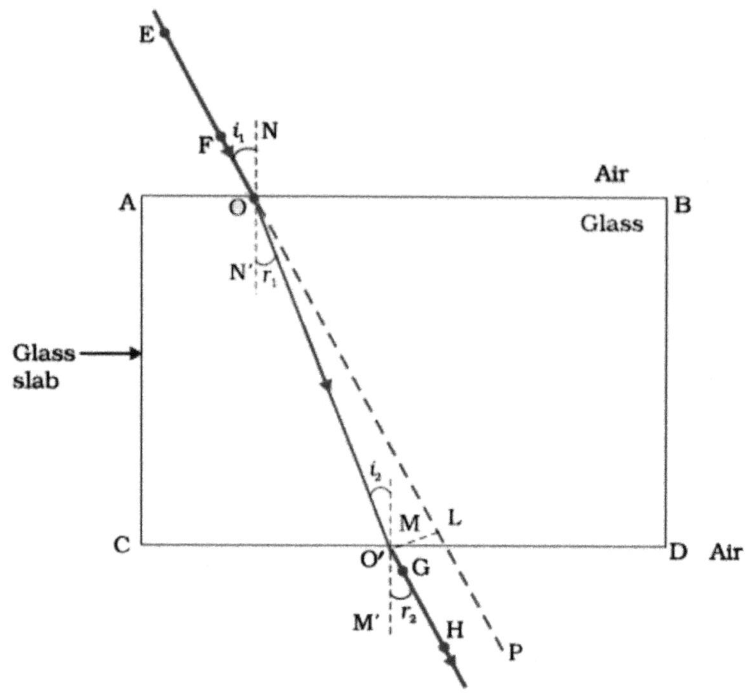

- When a ray of light of light enters the glass slab from air then we can notice that the ray of light bends towards the normal. This happens due to refraction of light.

- This ray of light then escapes from glass to air and this time the ray of light bends away from the normal.

- The ray of light which emerges out of the slab is termed as emergent ray.

- The angle which the emergent ray makes with the normal is termed as angle of emergence.

- If the incident ray EO is produced forward then we can notice that this ray moves parallel with the emergent ray.

- The perpendicular distance between incident ray produced froward and emergent ray is termed as *Lateral displacement.* It depends on *thickness of the glass slab, angle of incidence, refractive index and wavelength of light.*

Refraction by Spherical lenses

Lens is a transparent material which is bound by two surfaces. One or both the surfaces are spherical. There are different types of lens but we are going to study only about Convex and Concave lens in this chapter.

Convex lens	Concave lens
They have both the spherical surfaces bulged outwards	They have both the spherical surfaces bulged inwards.
They are thicker at the middle and thinner at the edges	They are thinner at the middle and thicker at the edges.
They are also known as converging lens.	They are also known as diverging lens.

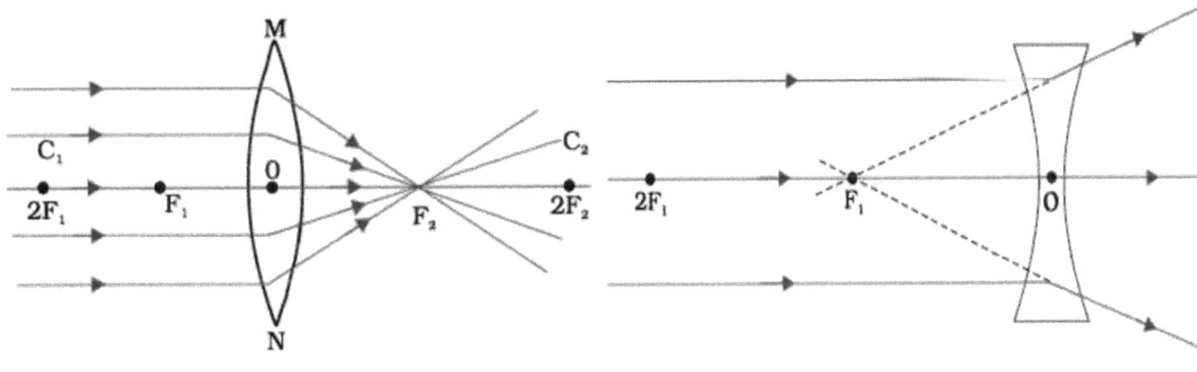

CONVERGING ACTION OF CONVEX LENS   DIVERGING ACTION OF CONVEX LENS

Terms associated with lens:

1. **Centre of curvature:** A lens has two imaginary spherical surfaces. The centre of these spherical surfaces are called centre of curvature. Since there are two spherical surfaces so there are two centre of curvature as well termed as C_1 and C_2.

2. **Optical centre:** The geometrical centre of the lens is called optical centre. A ray of light passing through the optical centre suffers minimum deviation and since this deviation is minimum we tend to say that it passes straight without any bending.

3. **Principal axis:** It is an imaginary line joining both the centre of curvature by passing through the optical centre.

4. **Aperture:** The diameter of the reflecting surface of the spherical mirror is called Aperture.

5. **Principal focus:** It is a point on the principal axis which is equidistant from centre of curvature and optical centre. If a ray of light is parallel to the principal axis then after striking the lens it either passes or it appears to pass through Principal focus.

6. **Focal length:** It is the distance between principal focus and the optical centre.

7. **Radius of curvature:** It is the distance between optical centre and centre of curvature. It is two times the focal length.

Ray diagrams:

With the changing position of the object with respect to the lens, images will be formed at different positions. We draw the ray diagram to find out the position of the image with respect to the position of the object.

But before making the ray diagrams we need to understand the pattern how a ray of light passes through a lens.

1. If a ray of light passes parallel to the principal axis then after refraction it either passes through the principal focus or it appears to pass through the principal focus.

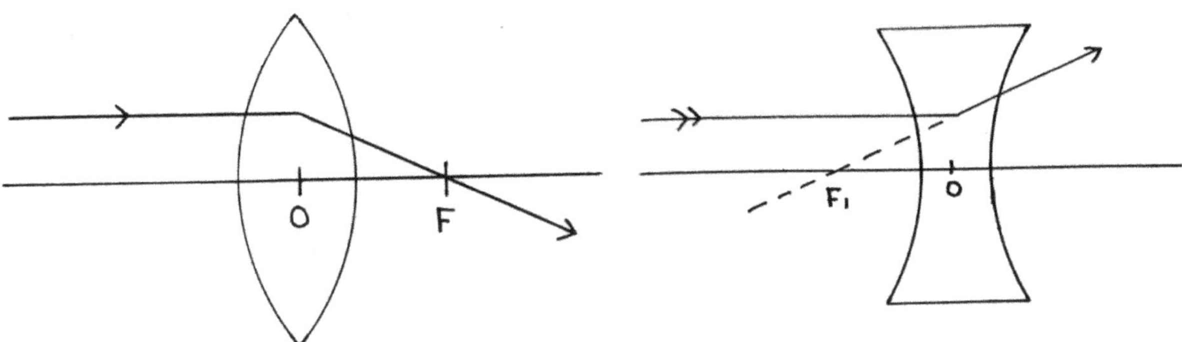

2. If a ray of light either passes or appears to pass through the focus then after refraction through the lens it becomes parallel to the principal axis.

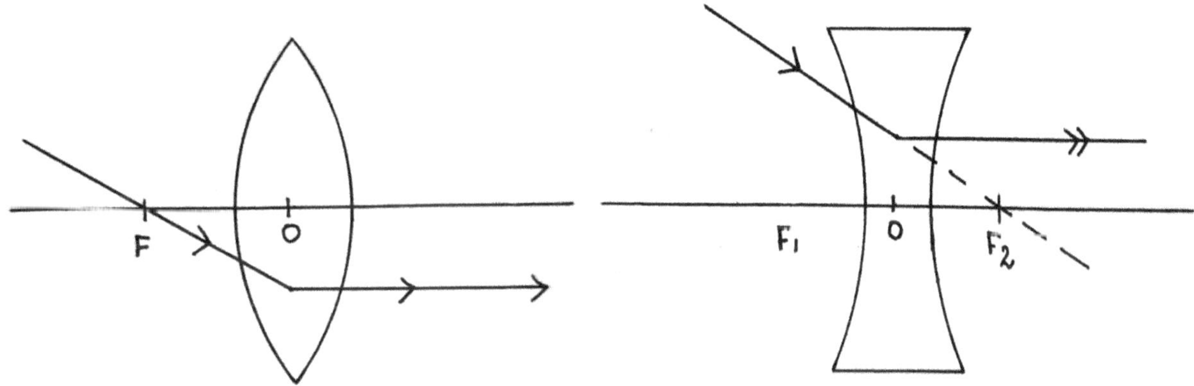

3. If a ray of light passes through the optical centre of the lens then it passes without any deviation.

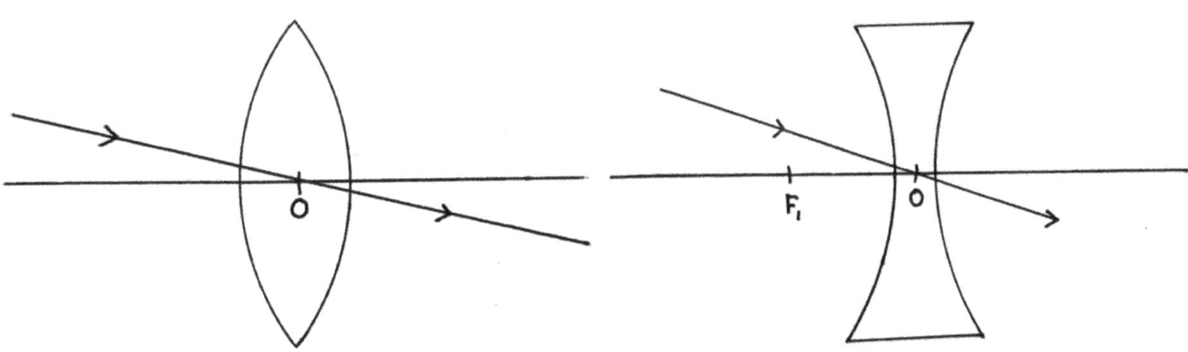

Image formation of Convex lens:

Case 1: When the object is at infinity

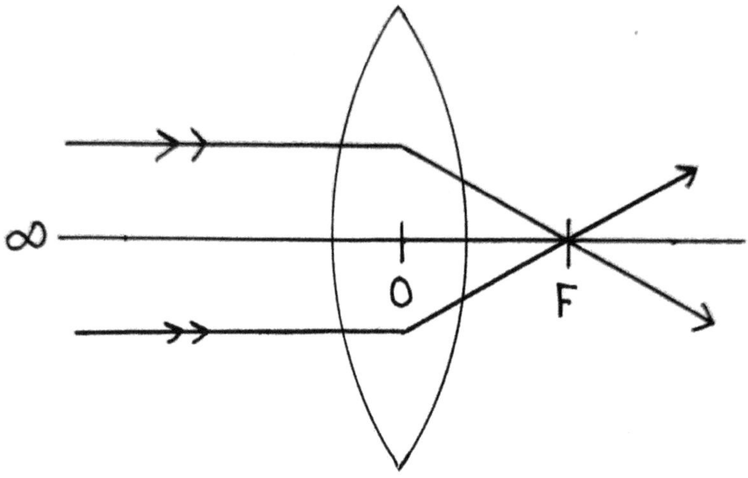

Properties of image:

a. Image is real and inverted

b. Size of the image is highly diminished

c. Image is formed at focus.

Case 2: When the object is beyond 2F

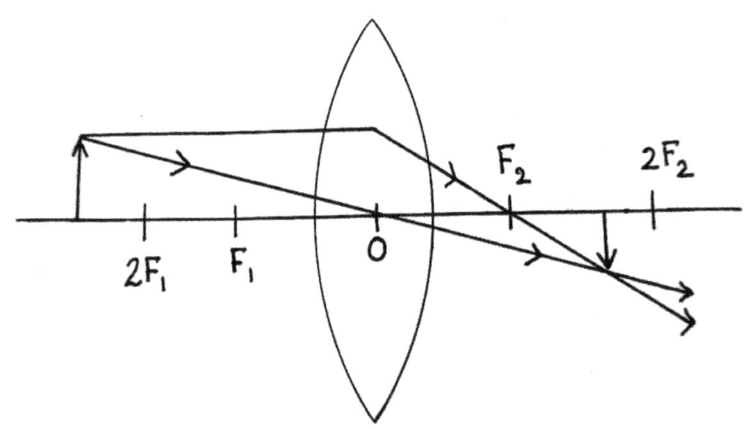

Properties of the image:

a. Image is real and inverted

b. Size of the image is diminished

c. Image is formed between focus and 2F.

Case 3: When the object is at 2F

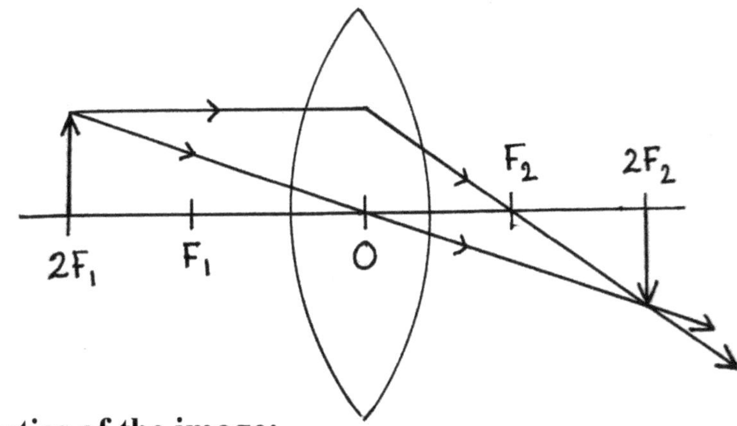

Properties of the image:

a. Image is real and inverted

b. Size of the image is same as that of the object

c. Image is formed at 2F.

Case 4: When the object is between 2F and focus

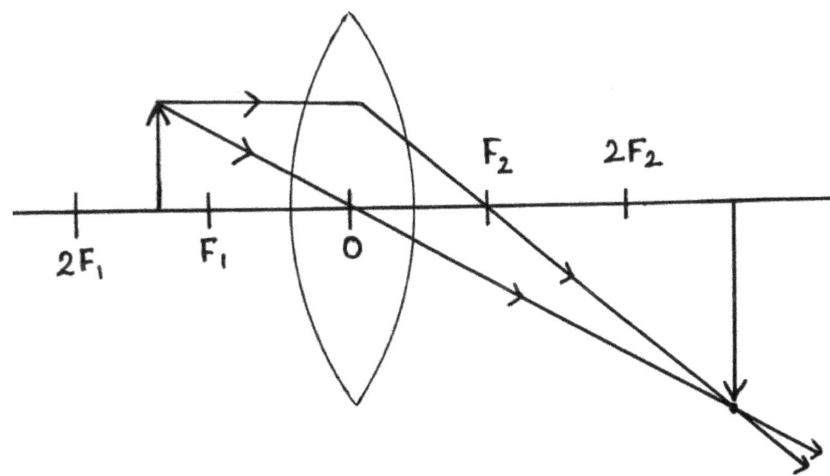

Properties of the image:

a. Image is real and inverted

b. Size of the image is enlarged

c. Image is formed beyond 2F.

Case 5: When the object is at focus

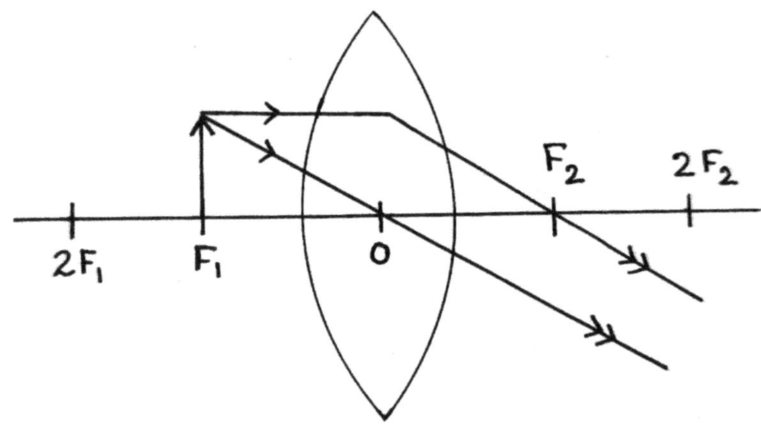

Properties of the image:

a. Image is real and inverted

b. Size of the image is highly enlarged

c. Image is formed at infinity.

Note:

In all the above 5 cases we can see that a real image is formed.

Case 6: When the object is between focus and optical centre

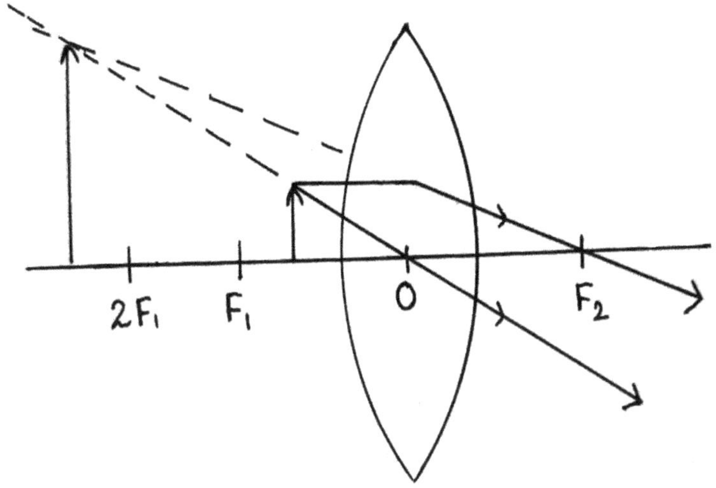

Properties of the image:

a. Image is virtual and erect

b. Size of the image is enlarged

c. Image appears to form at at the same side of the object.

Note: This is the only case where a virtual image is formed using a convex lens.

Trick to remember ray diagram of convex lens

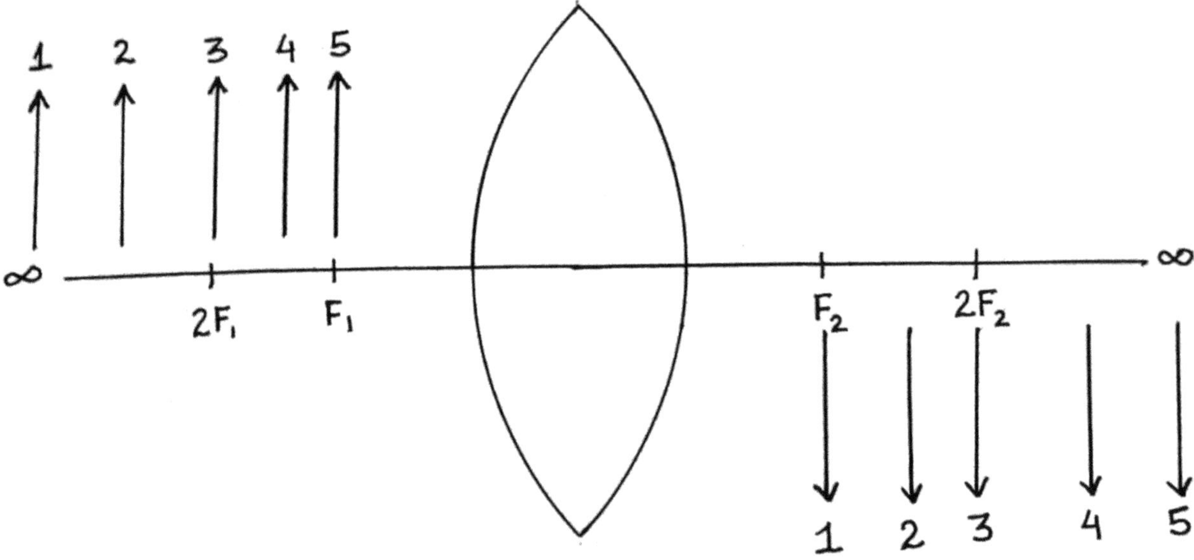

If you look at the diagram carefully you will notice that the numbers 1 – 5 at the left end of the diagram represents the different position of the object.

The numbers 1 – 5 at the right end of the diagram represents the different positions of the image.

All you need to remember is that same numbers at the left and right side of the lens represents the respective position of the object and the image.

For example: Junction 2 at the left end of the lens matches with junction 2 at the right side of the lens. This shows that if the object is at junction 2 then its image will be at junction 2 situated at the right side of the lens. Here junction 2 at the left side of the lens represents the position of the object beyond centre of curvature and the junction 2 at the right side of the lens represents the position of the image between focus and centre of curvature. This means that if the object is beyond centre of curvature then its image will be formed between focus and centre of curvature.

In this way you can remember the relative positions of object and image before making the ray diagrams.

Question: *Can you guess where will the image be formed if an object is positioned at the focus of the convex lens?*

Image formation by Concave lens

Case 1: When the object is at infinity

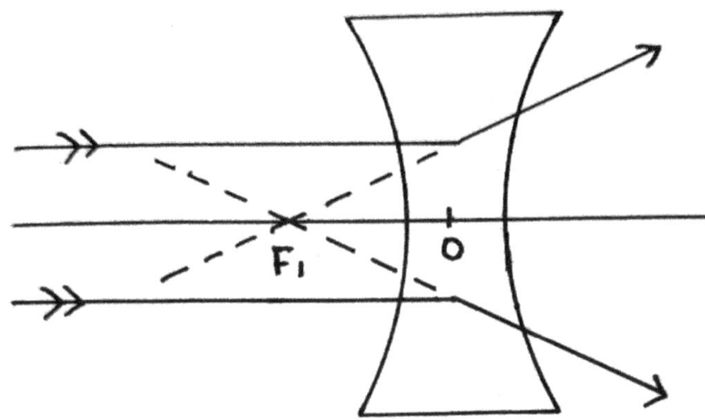

Properties of the image:

a. Image is virtual and erect.

b. Size of the image is highly diminished

c. Image appears to form at focus on the same side of the object.

Case 2: When the object is at a finite distance

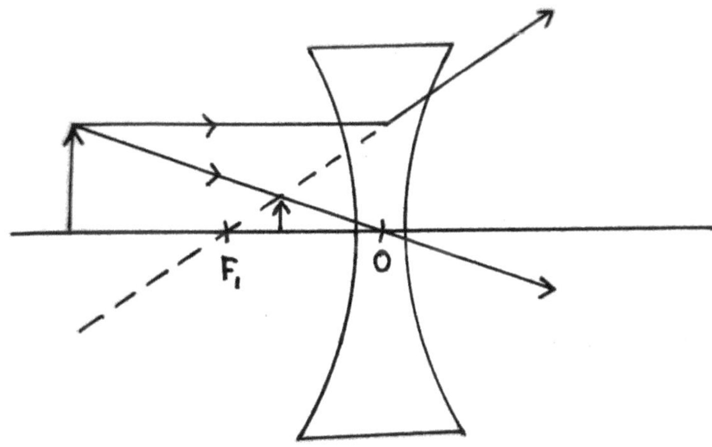

Properties of the image:

a. Image is virtual and erect

b. Size of the image is diminished

c. Image appears to form between focus and optical centre on the same side of the object.

Sign convention of the spherical lens:

While doing the calculations related to the spherical lens we shall follow the Cartesian Sign convention system. Here are the key points:

a. The optical centre of the lens is supposed to be the origin.

b. The principal axis is supposed to be the x – axis.

c. The object shall always be kept to the left side of the lens and light from the object must fall on the lens from the left side only.

d. All the measurements to the right of the optical centre are taken as positive and all the measurements to the left of the optical centre are taken as negative.

e. All the measurements above the principal axis are taken as positive and all the measurements below the principal axis are taken negative.

Note: Since the focal length of the convex lens is taken on the right side of the optical centre we will assume its value to be positive and since the focal length of the concave lens is taken on the right side of the optical centre we will assume its value to be negative.

Focal length of concave lens = negative

Focal length of convex lens = positive

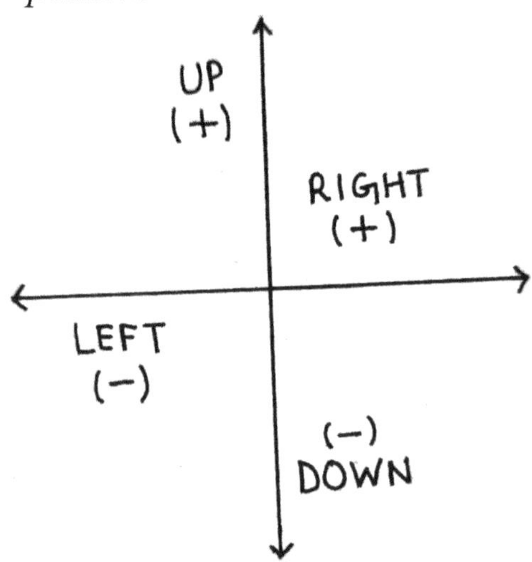

Lens Formula

In case of a spherical lens

u = distance of the object from the lens

v = distance of the image from the lens

f = focal length

and thus the lens formula is:

$$\frac{1}{f} = \frac{1}{v} - \frac{1}{u}$$

Magnification:

Magnification of the image can be defined as the ratio of height of the image to height of the object.

$$m = \frac{height\ of\ the\ image}{height\ of\ the\ object}$$

There is one more formula of magnification which is :

$$m = \frac{v}{u}$$

Note: The values placed in the magnification and lens formula must be placed **"along with the signs"** as per the sign convention.

Example:

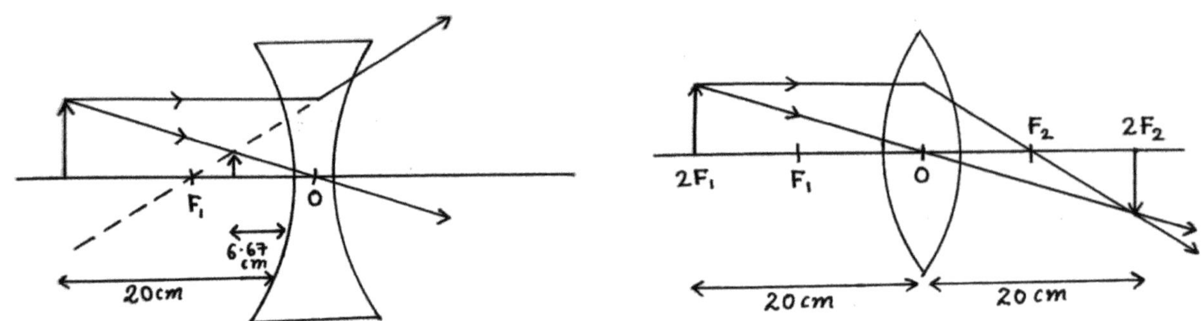

In the above diagram the values will be as follows:

Case 1: Concave spherical lens

f = - 10 cm

u = - 20 cm

v = -6.67 cm

m= (-6.67/-20) = 0.33

Case 2: Convex spherical lens

f = 10 cm

u = - 20 cm

v = 20cm

m = (20 / -20) = -1

- Case 1 shows that the value of magnification is 0.33 which is equal to 1/3. Since the value is in positive that shows that the image is virtual in nature. Also 1/3 indicates that the size of the image is 3 times diminished than the object.

- Case 2 shows that the value of magnification is -1. Since the value is in negative that shows that the image is real in nature. Also 1 indicates that the image will be of the same size as that of the object.

Examples:

1. In case of a convex lens of focal length 10cm an object is placed at a distance of 25cm. Find out the position of image with respect to the lens. Also find out the magnification of the image.

Solution:

Since it's a convex lens therefore as per the sign convention positive sign will be used with focal length.

$F = 10cm$

$u = -25cm$

$v = ?$

using lens formula:

$$\frac{1}{f} = \frac{1}{v} - \frac{1}{u}$$

Let's substitute the values now:

$$\frac{1}{10} = \frac{1}{v} - \frac{1}{-25}$$

$$\frac{1}{10} = \frac{1}{v} + \frac{1}{25}$$

$$\frac{1}{10} - \frac{1}{25} = \frac{1}{v}$$

$$\frac{5-2}{50} = \frac{1}{v}$$ (the L.C.M. of 25 and 10 is 50)

$$\frac{3}{50} = \frac{1}{v}$$ (the reciprocal of this value will give us the value of 'v')

$$v = \frac{50}{3} \text{cm}$$

Now let's calculate magnification

$$m = \frac{v}{u}$$

$$m = \frac{50/3}{-25}$$

$$m = -\frac{50}{3 \times 25}$$

$$m = -\frac{2}{3}$$

- This value of the magnification indicates that the size of the image is two-third of the size of the object. The minus sign in the magnification means that the image is real and inverted in nature.

2. In case of a concave lens of focal length 15cm an object is placed at a distance of 30cm. Find out the position of image with respect to the lens. Also find out the magnification of the image.

Solution:

Since it's a concave lens therefore as per the sign convention negative sign will be used with focal length.

F = -15cm

u = -30cm

v = ?

using lens formula:

$$\frac{1}{f} = \frac{1}{v} - \frac{1}{u}$$

$$\frac{1}{-15} = \frac{1}{v} - \frac{1}{-30}$$

$$\frac{1}{-15} = \frac{1}{v} + \frac{1}{30}$$

$$\frac{1}{-15} - \frac{1}{30} = \frac{1}{v} \quad \text{(the L.C.M. of 15 and 30 is 30)}$$

$$\frac{-2-1}{30} = \frac{1}{v}$$

$$\frac{-3}{30} = \frac{1}{v}$$

$$\frac{-1}{10} = \frac{1}{v}$$

$v = -10cm$

(The negative value of v indicates the image will be formed on the left side i.e. on the same side of the object in front of the lens)

Now let's calculate the value of magnification

$$m = \frac{v}{u}$$

$$m = \frac{-10}{-30}$$

$$m = \frac{1}{3}$$

- The value of magnification shows that the image will be one-third the size of the object. Since the magnification is positive, it shows that the image is virtual and erect.

Power of lens

- Power of lens is defined as the degree of convergence or divergence achieved by the lens.
- It's SI unit is 'dioptre' (D).
- Power of lens has an inverse relationship with the focal length of the lens i.e. more the focal length lesser is the power.

Formula:

$$P = \frac{1}{f}$$

In the above formula:

P indicates Power of lens

f indicates focal length of the lens(*in metres*).

Example: If the focal length of a lens is 0.25m then its power will be:

$$P = \frac{1}{f}$$

$$P = \frac{1}{0.25}$$

$$P = 4D$$

- Power of lens shows '***additive property***'.
  This means that the net power of multiple lenses will be the algebraic sum of individual powers.

For example of three lenses of power 2D, -3D and 0.25D are combined together to act like a single lens then the net power will be:

$P = P_1 + P_2 + P_3$

$P = 2 + (-3) + 0.25$

$P = -0.75D$

- Thick lens have less focal length and thus have more Power. Opposite to this, thin lens have more focal length and thus have less power.
  Now can you correlate why old age people have thick lens in their spectacles?

- If the power of a lens is in negative then that means that the focal length will also be negative and if the power of a lens is in positive then that means that the focal length will also be positive. Now you need to remember that which type of lens will have positive focal length and which one will have negative focal length.

Question: Two lenses having focal length – 3D and 2.5D are combined together to act like a single lens.

a. Identify the type of lens.

b. Calculate the Net power.

Answer:

a. Since the power of first lens is negative then that indicates that the focal length of this lens is also negative and as per the sign convention Concave lens have negative focal length. Also, Convex lens tends to have positive focal length therefore the second lens is convex.

b. $P = P_1 + P_2$

$P = -3D + 2.5D$

$P = -0.5D$

The net power is -0.5D thus we can also conclude that the lens will tend to behave like Concave lens.

Uses of Spherical lens

Convex lens:

1. It is used as a Magnifying glass.

2. It is used as eye correction glass.

3. It is used in telescope.

4. It is used in projectors.

Magnifying lens

Concave lens:

1. It is used as spy lens at doors.

2. It is used as eye correction glass.

3. They are used in scanner machines to widen the laser beam so that it can access a specific area.

4. They are used in flash lights to diverge the rays from the other side.

Spy lens

- Light travels in a straight line.

- Images can be real or virtual depending on the type of mirror or lens used. It also depends on the position of object.

- Mirror formula gives the relationship between distance of the object (u), distance of the image (v) and the focal length (f).

- Radius of curvature is double the focal length.

- Magnification is the ratio of height of the image and the height of the object.

- Light travelling from denser to rarer medium bends away from the normal and light travelling from rarer to denser medium bends towards the normal.

- Speed of light is different in different medium.

- Refractive index is the ratio of speed of light in vacuum/air to speed of light in the given medium.

- Power of lens is the reciprocal of focal length.

- SI unit of power of a lens is dioptre.

- Thin lens will have less power since their focal length is more. Thick lens will have more power since their focal length is less.

Question 1. Define the principal focus of a concave mirror.

Answer 1: When a ray of light passes parallel to the principal axis then after reflection it passes through a point on the principal axis known as Principal focus. Also, Focus is a point on the principal axis which is equidistant from pole and centre of curvature.

Question 2: The radius of curvature of a spherical mirror is 20cm. What is its focal length?

Answer 2: Since focal length is half of radius of curvature so it would be 10cm.

Question 3: Name a mirror that can give an erect and enlarged image of an object.

Answer 3: Concave mirror.

Question 4: Why do we prefer a convex mirror as a rear view mirror in vehicles?

Answer 4: Convex mirror gives a wider field of view by producing diminished image and that is why it is preferred as a rear view mirror.

Question 5: Find the focal length of a convex mirror whose radius of curvature is 32cm.

Answer 5: 16cm.

Question 6: A concave mirror produces three times magnified real image of an object placed at 10cm in front of it. Where is the image located?

Answer 6: We will use the formula of magnification here:

$$m = \frac{-v}{u}$$

In the question it is mentioned that the image is three times magnified and real so, m = - 3

u = - 10 cm

Substituting the value in the formula we get,

$$-3 = \frac{-v}{-10}$$

v= - 30 cm

Question 7: A ray of light travelling in air enters obliquely into water. Does the light ray bend towards the normal or away from the normal? Why?

Answer 7: Air is a rarer medium while water is denser than air and when light travels from rarer to denser medium it bends towards the normal. This is because the speed of light decreases when a ray travels from rarer to denser medium.

Question 8: Light enters from air to glass having refractive index 1.50. What is the speed of light in the glass? The speed of light in vacuum is 3 x 10^8 m/s.

Answer 8:

$$\mu = \frac{c}{v} = \frac{3 \times 10^8}{v}$$

$$1.5 = \frac{3 \times 10^8}{v}$$

$$v = \frac{3 \times 10^8}{1.5}$$

v = 2 x 10^8 m/s.

Question 9: Find out from the table the medium having highest optical density. Also find the medium with lowest optical density.

Medium	Refractive index	Material	Refractive index
Air	1.0003	Canada balsam	1.53
Ice	1.31	Rock salt	1.54
Water	1.33	Carbon disulphate	1.63
Alcohol	1.36	Dense flint glass	1.65
Kerosene	1.44	Ruby	1.71
Fused quart	1.46	Sapphire	1.77
Turpentine oil	1.47	Diamond	2.42
Benzene	1.50		
Crown glass	1.52		

Answer 9: Medium having lowest optical density is Air and the medium having highest optical density is Diamond.

Question 10: You are given kerosene, turpentine and water. In which of these does the light travel fastest?

Answer 10: The speed of light will be maximum in water since its Refractive index is minimum.

Question 11: The refractive index of diamond is 2.42. What do you mean by this statement?

Answer 11: This statement means that the speed of light in diamond will be 2.42 times slower as compared to that in air.

Question 12: Define 1 dioptre power of lens.

Answer 12: 1 dioptre is defined as the power of lens whose focal length is 1 meter.

Question 13: A convex lens forms a real and inverted image of a needle at a distance of 50 cm from it. Where is the needle placed in front of the convex lens if the image is equal to the size of the object? Also find out the power of lens.

Answer 13: Since the size of the image and the object is same it is evident that the object is placed at 2F. The distance of the object will also be equal to 50 cm forms the lens.

Since the value of 2F is 50 cm the focal length will be 25 cm or 0.25m. Power of lens will be reciprocal of focal length so its value will be $\dfrac{1}{0.25}$= 4D.

Question 14: Find the power of a concave lens of focal length 2 m.

Answer 14: Since it is concave lens so as per the sign convention focal length will be (- 2)

$$\text{Power} = \dfrac{1}{focal\ length}$$

$$P = \dfrac{1}{-2} = \text{-0.5 D}$$

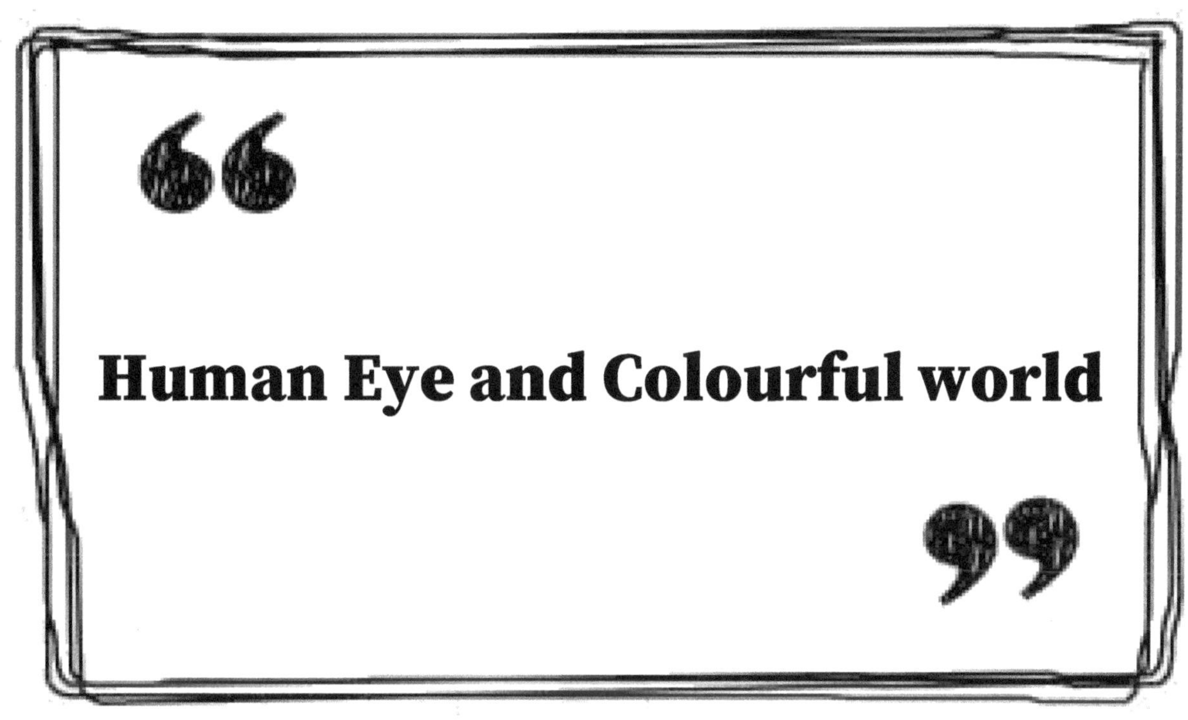

Human Eye and Colourful world

Chapter: Human eye and the colourful world

Parts of Human eye:

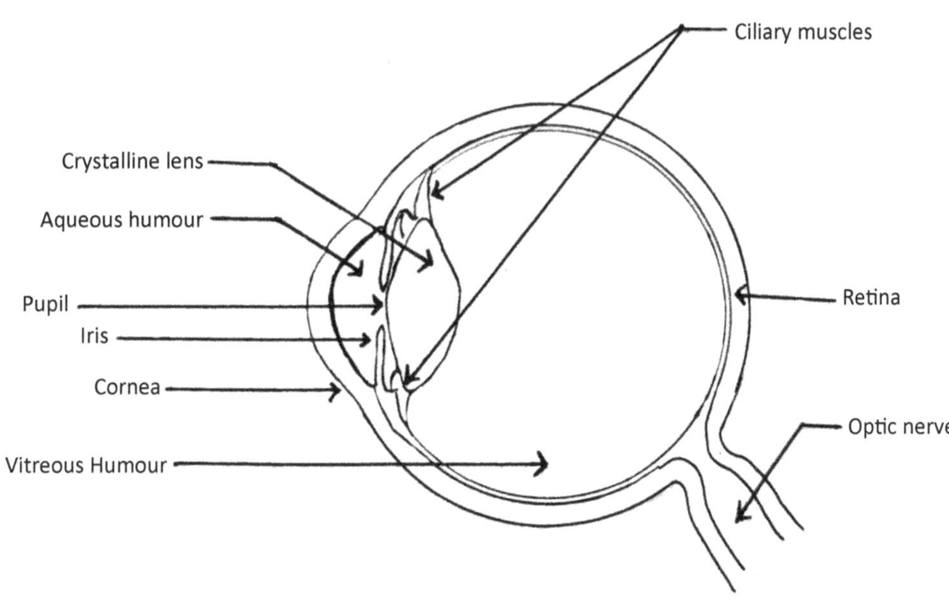

1. **Crystalline lens:** Human eye is provided with a convex lens. It provides fine adjustment of focal length which is required to focus the objects at different distance.

2. **Cornea:** Light enters the eye through cornea. It is the outermost bulged portion of the human eye. Most of the refraction takes place here.

3. **Pupil**: It controls the amount of light entering the human eye.

4. **Iris:** It is the dark muscular diaphragm which controls the size of the pupil. It is also the part which is responsible for the colour of our eyes.

5. **Retina:** It is a membrane with a large number of light sensitive cells which gets activated upon illumination and then creates an electrical signal which is sent to the brain through optic nerves. The brain thus interprets the signal and perceive the object.

6. **Ciliary muscle:** It helps in changing the shape of the lens. The curvature of the lens can be modified with the help of ciliary muscles.

7. **Aqueous humour:** It is the watery liquid in the front part of the eye which provides nutrition to the lens.

8. **Vitreous humour:** It helps to keep the eye in shape and also provides nutrients. It is present between lens and retina.

How do our eyes adjust to see near and far object?

Ciliary muscles changes the curvature of the lens and with the change in curvature the focal length of the lens also changes. When the muscles are relaxed, the lens becomes thinner and subsequently its focal length increases and that's how we are able to see distant objects. When the muscles contracts, the lens becomes thicker and its focal length decreases and that's how we are able to see near objects. This property of the eye to adjust its focal length as per its need is called the **Power of accommodation.**

Near point of the eye: It is the minimum distance from the eye at which an object can be most distinctly seen. It is about 25 cm for human eye.

Far point of the eye: It is the farthest point up to which a human eye can see objects clearly. For a human eye the far point is set at infinity.

How do our eyes adjust between high and low light?

Pupil controls the amount the light needed by the eye with the help of Iris. When we are looking at a bright object then iris reduce the size of the pupil which allows lesser light to enter. Now just after this if you go to a room where the lights are dim you would realise that you are not able to see things properly and that is why your eyes needs to adjust by expanding the pupil to allow more light to come.

Defects in human eye

There are four common eye defects in humans. Lets discuss about these defects along with their correction.

a.   Myopia

- Myopia also known as near sightedness is a common eye defect.
- People suffering from this defect are able to see near objects clearly but they are not able to see distant objects clearly.
- They are able to see only up to a few metres.
- The far point of the eye in this case is less than infinity.
- In this defect the rays are focussed in front of the retina instead of the retina itself.
- **Reason:**
  1. Elongation of the eye ball.

  2. Excessive curvature of the eye lens which decreases the focal length.

- **Correction:** It can be corrected using a Concave lens.

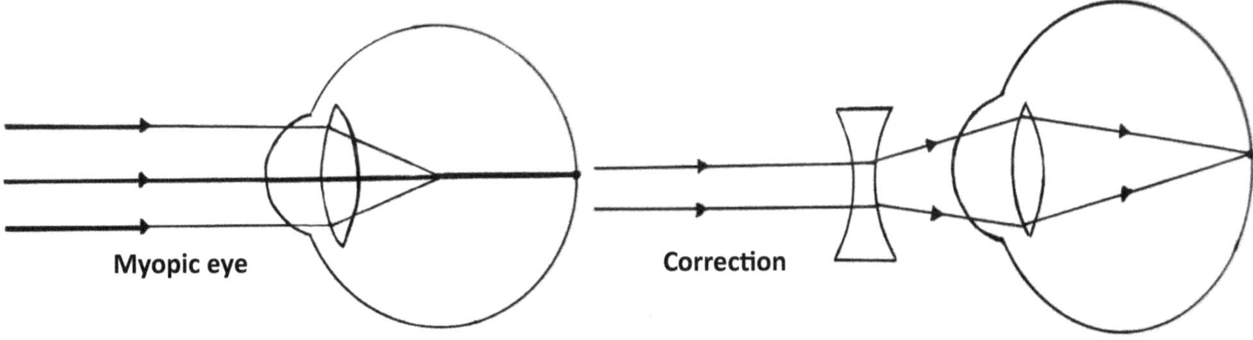

b. Hypermetropia

- Hypermetropia is also known as far sightedness.
- People suffering from this defect are able to see far objects clearly but they are not able to see near objects clearly.
- The near point of the eye in this case is beyond 25 cm.
- In this defect the rays are focussed at a point behind the retina instead of the retina itself.
- **Reason:**
  1. The eyeball is too small.
  2. Little curvature of the eye lens which increases the focal length.
- **Correction:** It can be corrected using a convex lens.

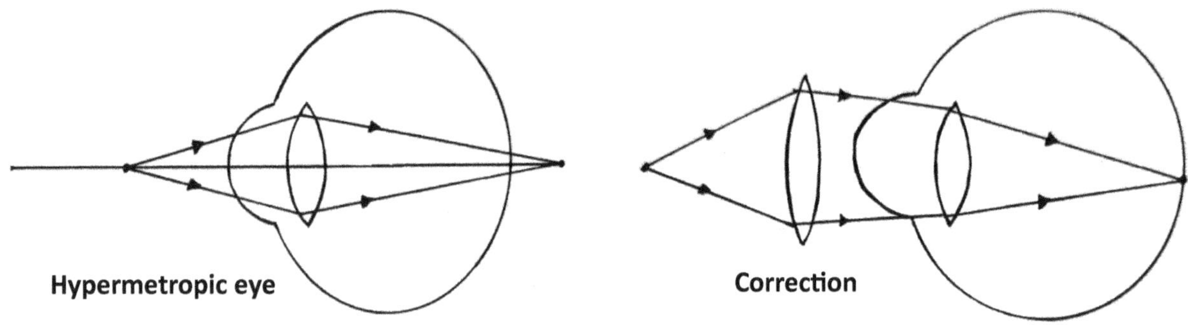

c. Presbyopia

- It is an ageing effect.
- In this defect the power of accommodation of the eye decreases.
- It affects the eyes ability to focus on nearby objects.
- This defect is also known as Old age Hypermetropia.
- In this type of eye defect a person might suffer from both myopia and hypermetropia.
- **Reason:** Gradual weakening of ciliary muscles.
- **Correction:** Convex or Bifocal lens.

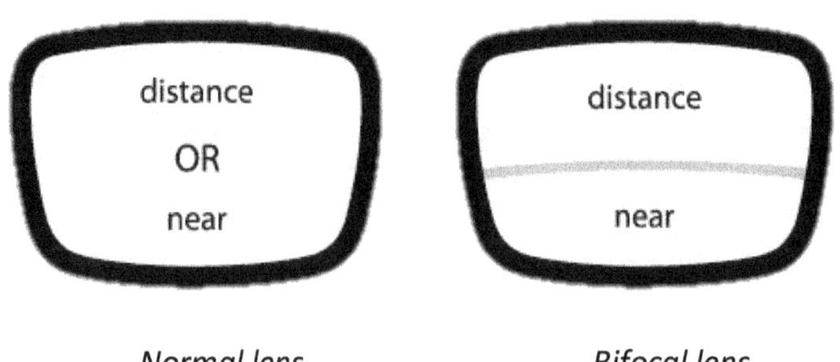

Normal lens   *Bifocal lens*

d. Cataract:

- It generally happens in old age.
- In this type of defect the lens become cloudy.
- People suffering from this may suffer partial or complete loss of vision.
- It can be corrected only through a surgery.

Colour Vision

Our eye has light sensitive cells of two shapes – rods and cones.
The rod shaped cells respond to the intensity of light or degree of brightness or darkness. They do not perceive colour or fine details. The cone shaped cells respond to the colours and help us to differentiate between colours. When a person is not able to distinguish between certain colours he/she is said to be **Colour Blind**. This defect is generally inherited from parents to their children. This happens when a person may not have a particular kind of cones on its retina and as a result his/her eye will not be sensitive to a certain colour.

Eye transplant

After the death of a person, if the eye is removed and donated in an eye bank within 4-6 hours then it **could** help a blind people. Eye Blindness in people is due to multiple reasons but in most of the cases there is a problem in cornea of the eye. A part of the corneal tissue from the donated eye is used to replace the defected cornea.

Process of eye transplantation:
1. Eye is donated.
2. Donor's eyes are then sent to an eye bank.
3. The eye bank evaluates the cornea for suitability.
4. If suitable, the cornea is prepared for transplantation.
5. The recipient undergoes cornea transplant surgery.
6. After surgery, the recipient regains or improves their vision.

Numericals based on lens formula:

Tips to solve numericals of lens formula which involves the concept of human eye:
- For a person suffering from Hypermetropia, his near point of vision is defected.
- For a person suffering from Myopia, his far point of vision is defected.
- For a person suffering from **_Hypermetropia_** his defected near point of vision will be considered as 'v' and the near point of normal eye will be considered as 'u'. Suppose a person is suffering from Hypermetropia and the near point of this person is 50 cm while the near point of normal human eye is 25 cm. In this case v = -50 cm and u = -25 cm.

- For a person suffering from **_Myopia_** his defected far point of vision will be considered as 'v' and the far point of normal eye will be considered as 'u'.Suppose a person is suffering from Myopia and the far point of this person is 100 cm while the far point of normal human eye is infinity. In this case v = -100 cm and u = ∞

- Also keep a check on the sign convention and keep both the values of u and v as negative.

- While doing the numericals if a calculation comes in between where we need to find the value of $\frac{1}{\infty}$ then you can consider this value as zero and neglect it.

Example 1: A person is suffering from Hypermetropia and his near point of vision is 100 cm. He needs to correct his defect with the help of a lens. If the near point of normal eye is 25 cm then calculate the power of lens required to correct this eye defect.

Solution 1: Given:

u = - 25 cm

v = - 100 cm

using the lens formula we know that:

$$\frac{1}{f} = \frac{1}{v} - \frac{1}{u}$$

$$\frac{1}{f} = \frac{1}{-100} - \frac{1}{-25}$$

$$\frac{1}{f} = \frac{3}{100}$$

$$f = \frac{100}{3} \text{ cm or } \frac{1}{3} \text{ m}$$

$$P = \frac{1}{f}$$

P = + 3 D

Example 2: The far point of a person suffering from myopia is 80 cm. What is the power of lens required by him?

Solution: Given -
v = - 80 cm
u = ∞

using the lens formula:

$$\frac{1}{f} = \frac{1}{v} - \frac{1}{u}$$

$$\frac{1}{f} = \frac{1}{-80} - \frac{1}{\infty}$$

but $\dfrac{1}{\infty} = 0$

$$\frac{1}{f} = \frac{1}{-80} \text{ cm}$$

f = - 80 cm or 0.8 m

$$P = \frac{1}{f}$$

$$P = \frac{1}{-0.8}$$
P = - 1.25 D

Refraction of light through a prism

A prism a transparent object having two triangular and three rectangular surfaces. The rectangular surfaces are also called Refracting surfaces.

The refracting surface on which light is incident and the refracting surface from which the light emerges out of the prism is inclined at a specific angle. This angle is called Angle of Prism.

Angle of Prism and Angle of Deviation

If the emergent ray is produced backward and the incident ray is produced forward they meet at an angle which is called Angle of Deviation.

We can clearly see in the diagram that the emergent ray is deviated with respect to the incident ray at a certain angle. This angle is called the Angle of Deviation.

Factors affecting angle of deviation:

- Angle of Incidence
- Angle of Prism
- Refractive Index
- Colour/Wavelength of light

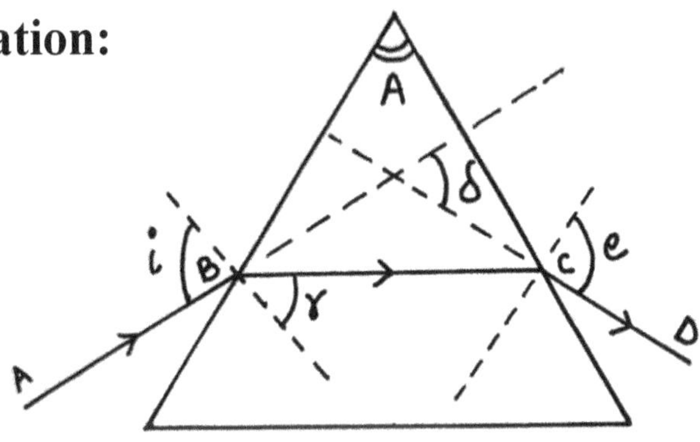

What is Dispersion of Light?

When a white light is incident on a glass prism then it splits into its constituent colours. This phenomenon is called Dispersion of light.

Different colours of light travels with different speed in different media. As a result different colours of light bends at different angles when they enter a new medium and as a result we get to see those colours. The band of light obtained after dispersion is called Spectrum. This band can be remembered with the help of the acronym ***VIBGYOR***.

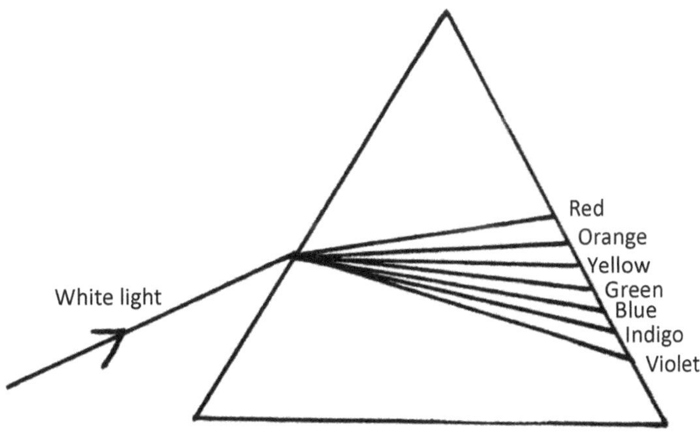

The red colour of light suffers minimum deviation and thus remains on the top whereas the violet colour of light suffers maximum deviation and remain at the bottom. It is to be remembered that the deviation of a colour of light depends on its wavelength.
Greater the wavelength of light, lesser is the deviation.

Newton's Experiment of Recombination

Sir Newton performed an experiment with the help of two identical prism. With the help of one prism he dispersed the white light into it's constituent colours. The dispersed light was then passed to the other prism which was kept at an inverted position. He noticed that the second prism recombined the dispersed light from the first prism into the white light again. This happened since the two prism where identical so the second prism produced the deviation at the same angle which helped in rejoining the dispersed light into the white light.

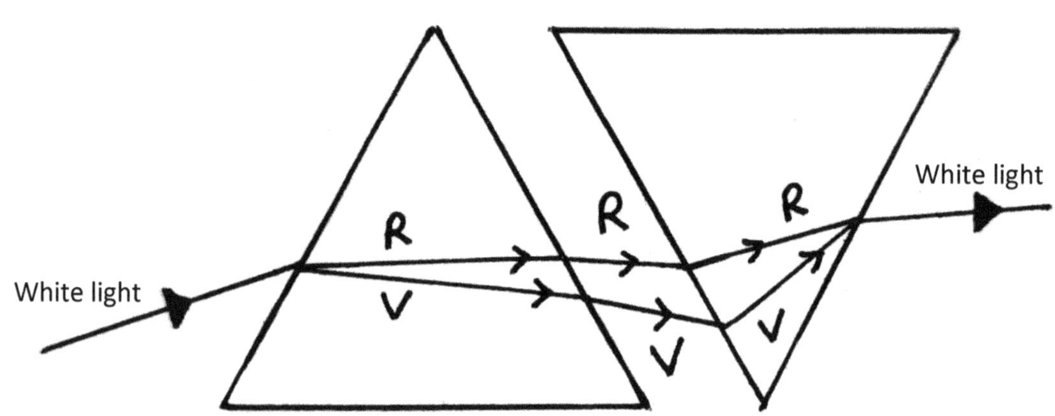

Internal Reflection

Before understanding the concept of Internal Reflection we need to understand the concept of critical angle.

What is critical angle?

When light travels from denser to rarer medium then there is a special angle of incidence in the denser medium with respect to which the angle of refraction in the rarer medium is 90^0. This angle is called Critical angle.

For a ray of light moving from denser to rarer medium :
a. The angle of incidence can be less than the critical angle
b. The angle of incidence can be equal to the critical angle
c. The angle of incidence can be greater than the critical angle.

- If the angle of incidence in the denser medium is less than the critical angle then refraction of light takes place. In this case most of the light gets refracted while a very small portion of light gets reflected as well.

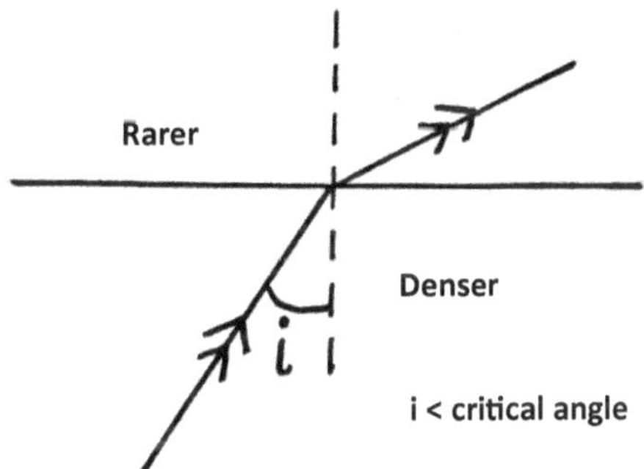

- If the angle of incidence in the denser medium is equal to the critical angle then light gets refracted in such a way that angle of refraction in the rarer medium is 90^0. This causes illumination of the surface at the interface of the two media.

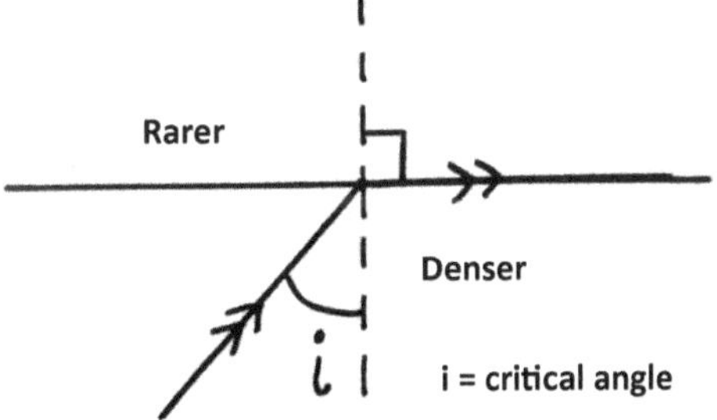

- If the angle of incidence in the denser medium is more than the critical angle then light gets internally reflected.

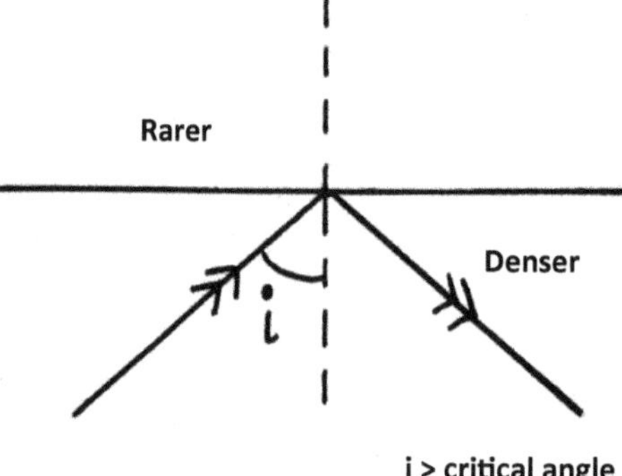

When a ray of light travels from an optically denser medium to an optically rarer medium with an angle of incidence greater than the critical angle then the light gets reflected back into the same medium. This phenomenon is called Internal Reflection.

The image formed by Internal reflection is brighter as compared to the image formed by Reflection of light. This is because in Reflection of light some portion of the light is scattered as well as refracted but in Internal Reflection all the light is reflected back thus the brightness of the image is more.

Conditions for Internal Reflection:

1. Light must pass from denser to rarer medium and not the vice versa.
2. The angle of incidence must be greater than the critical angle.

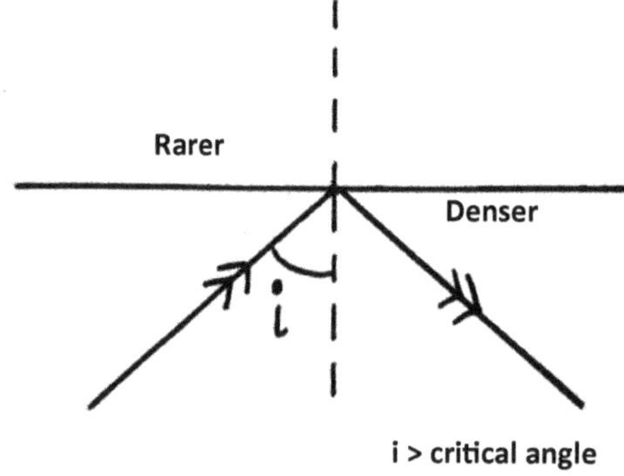

Note: *We need to remember that the critical angle is different for different pair of media. For example, the critical angle for light moving from glass to air is 42^0. This means that if ray of light is moving from glass to air with an angle of incidence greater than than 42^0 then it will get internally reflected.*

86

Formation of Rainbow

Formation of a rainbow is a natural phenomenon which generally happens after rainfall. The sunlight is dispersed with the help of tiny droplets which acts as mini prisms. The Spectrum thus obtained is the rainbow.

The sunlight first refracts when it enters the droplets and due to change of medium it gets dispersed. This dispersed light gets internally reflected and finally refracts out of the droplet. The phenomenon takes place simultaneously in millions of droplets and thus the spectrum thus formed constituted the rainbow. The red colour appears at the upper arc of the rainbow and the violet colour appears at the bottom.

Note: It is to the remembered that the rainbow is formed in the direction opposite to the sun.

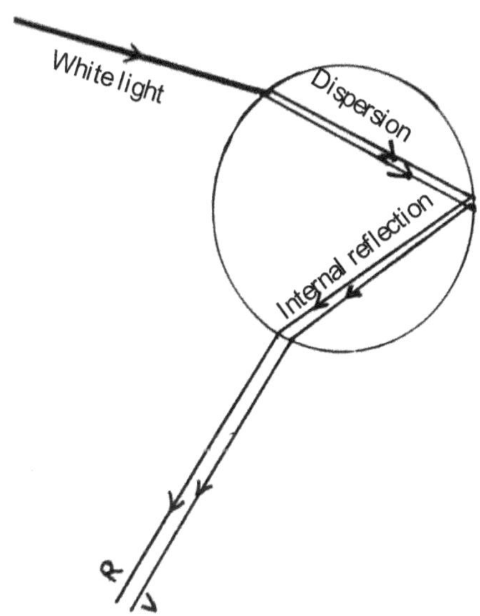

Atmospheric Refraction

The atmosphere can be divided into different layers. These layers have different air densities due to variation of temperature. Due to this, there is *slight variation* in the optical densities of different layers. Apparently, we can say that there is slight variation in the refractive indices of different layers.

When light passes through these layers there is slight change in the path of light which is called Atmospheric refraction.

Applications of Atmospheric refraction:

- Flickering of objects seen through a stream of hot air
- Stars appears slightly higher than the actual position.
- Twinkling of the stars.
- Advanced sunrise and delayed sunset.
- Apparent position of the sun.

Twinkling of the stars:

When light from stars reaches the earth atmosphere then it continuously passes through rarer and denser air. As a result light suffers bending from the original position which changes the apparent position of the star for a person viewing it from the earth's surface. As the light suffers successive refraction due to change in the refractive index at every layer the apparent position of the star suffers fluctuation which results in the twinkling effect of the star. Twinkling of star is also termed as *Astronomical Scintillation.*

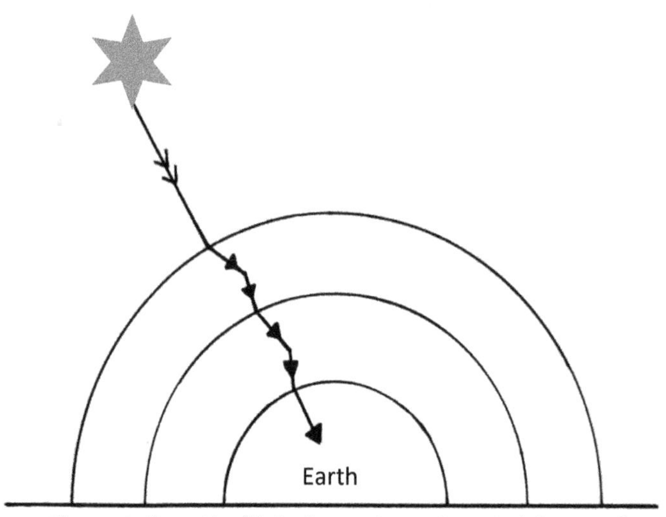

Change in the path of light due to change in optical density of warm and cold air in the atmosphere leading to twinkling effect

Scattering of light

Scattering of light is pretty different from reflection and refraction of light.
When light rays enters the atmosphere it meets very fine particles of the atmosphere due to which it spreads/reflect in ALL direction. This phenomenon of light is called Scattering of light.

Cause of Scattering of light:

When light strikes the fine particles of the atmosphere then the particle absorb some light and spread the rest in all the directions. This causes scattering of light.
We need to understand that when light meets these tiny particles then it gets absorbed and then gets re-emitted in all direction and this causes scattering of light.

Factors affecting scattering of light:
1. Wavelength of light: Greater the wavelength, lesser is the scattering of light.
2. Size of the particle: Greater the size of the particle, greater is the scattering of light.

Point to remember: *Since scattering of light depends on wavelength therefore the red colour of light suffers minimum scattering since its wavelength is maximum. At the same time you need to remember that the violet colour of light suffers maximum scattering since its wavelength is minimum.*

Some phenomenon based on scattering of light are:
- Tyndall effect
- Blue colour of the sky
- Red colour of the sky during sunrise and sunset

What is Tyndall Effect?

The earth's atmosphere consists of tiny particles. When light strikes these particles the path of light becomes illuminated and the particles become visible. The illumination of the path of light due to scattering of light is called Tyndall Effect. The phenomenon can be clearly seen in a room which is filled with dense smoke. When a strong beam of light is passed in this room the path of light becomes visible.

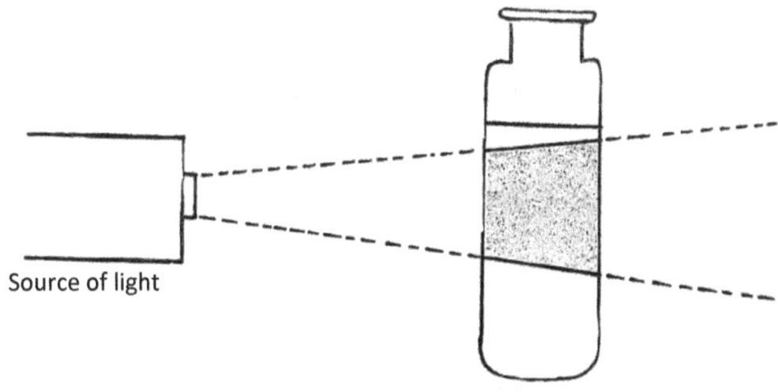

Scattering of light by relatively bigger particles

Do you know why the colour of sky is blue?

When light enters the earth's atmosphere it strikes the fine particles of the atmosphere which are typically smaller than the wavelength of the light. As a result the blue(violet, indigo, blue) colour of light gets scattered the most since its wavelength is minimum. The colour which scatters the most forms the colour of the sky.

Do you know why the sky appears red during sunrise and sunset?

During sunrise and sunset the distance between sun and earth is maximum and thus light has to travel through the thicker layers of the air. While passing through the atmosphere most of the light of lesser wavelength(blue, violet) gets scattered by the particles and therefore light of greater wavelength (red) reaches our eyes which forms the reddish appearance of the sun and the sky. Although at the noon time when the sun is overhead, the distance between sun and the earth is minimum due to which light suffers minimum scattering as only a little of the blue and the violet colours are scattered. Due to this the sky appears white during noon time.

What would be the colour of the sky when seen from the moon?

It would be all black. There's no atmosphere on the moon due to which there won't be any scattering of the light!

Do you know how sunscreen works?

Sunscreen works on the principal of scattering of light. The ingredients (usually zinc oxide and titanium dioxide) of sunscreen sit on top of the skin and thus blocks the UV ray to enter the skin and then scatter the rays.

CHAPTER AT A GLANCE – NCERT BASED IMPORTANT POINTS

- Most of the refraction in the human eye takes place in the cornea.
- By changing the focal length, the human eye can shift its focus between nearby and far objects.
- Myopia is also known as Near sightedness and can be corrected using a concave lens.
- Hypermetropia is also as Far sightedness and can be corrected using a convex lens.
- When a white lights enters a prism, it splits into its constituent colours and this is called Dispersion of light.
- The colour of sky appears to be blue because of scattering of light.
- Red colour of light has maximum wavelength and thus suffers minimum scattering.
- Stars appears to twinkle because of atmospheric refraction.

Question 1: What is meant by power of accommodation of the eye?

Answer 1: Our eye has the ability to shift its focus on objects at different distances. For this it has to do some adjustments in its lens by changing the shape of the lens with the help of the ciliary muscles. This ability of shifting its focus is known as the power of accommodation.

Question 2: A person with a myopic eye cannot see objects beyond 1.2 m distinctly. What should be the type of the corrective lens used to restore proper vision?

Answer 2: Since the defect is Myopia, concave lens of focal length 1.2 m must be used to restore the proper vision.

Question 3: What is the far point and near point of the human eye with normal vision?

Answer 3: For a person with normal vision the far point is infinity and the near point is around 25 cm.

Question 4: A student has difficulty reading the blackboard while sitting in the last row. What could be the defect the child is suffering from? How can it be corrected?

Answer 4: Since the child is not able to see far objects he must be suffering from myopia which could be corrected by using spectacles containing concave lens.

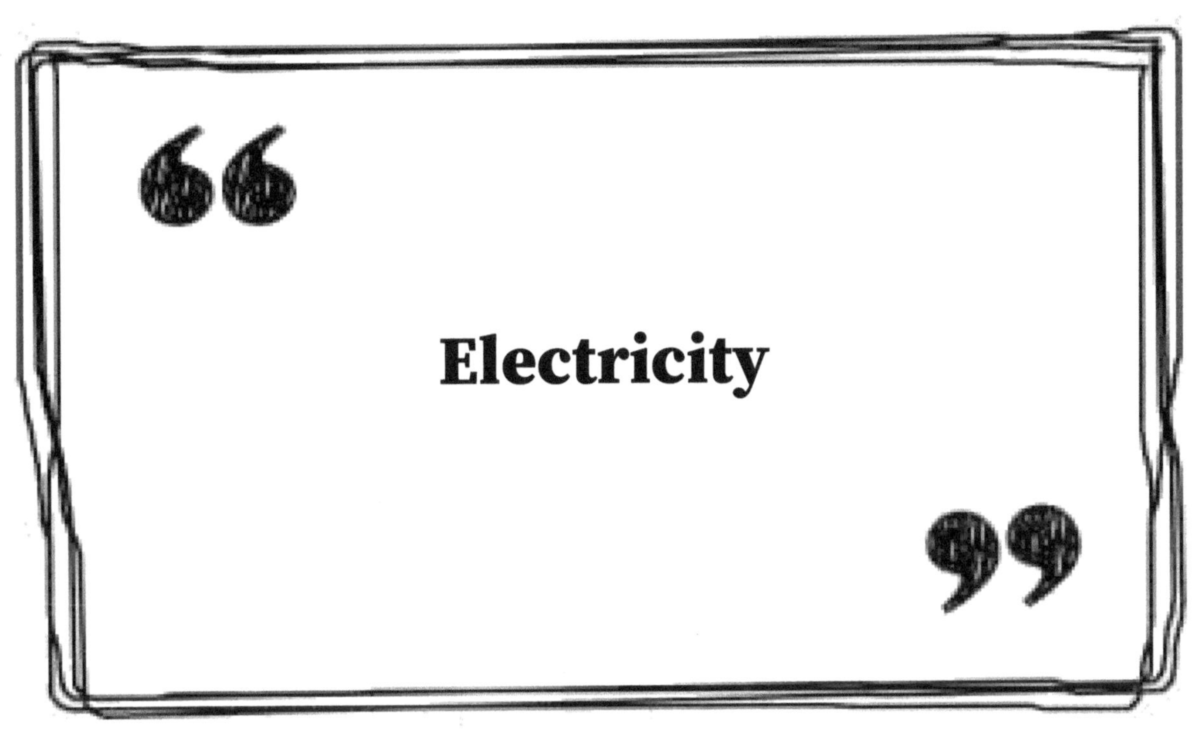

Electricity

Chapter: Electricity

What is Electric Charge?

Electric Charge is a physical property of matter.

The SI unit of charge is **Columb** (C) named after the French physicist Charles Augustin de Coulomb. Charges in the matter are carried out by the sub atomic particles. Negative charge is carried by Electrons and positive charge is carried by Protons.

The basic property of a charge is that when it is placed in an electromagnetic field it experiences a force which is known as Lorentz force.

The smallest possible charge is the magnitude of charge on one electron. This amount of charge is also termed as *'elementary charge'* which is about 1.602×10^{-19} C.

Charge exist in multiple of the charge on an electron.

If charge is denoted by the letter 'q' then:

$$q = n.e$$

where 'n' denotes number of electron and 'e' denotes the charge on one electron.

Always remember that mass can exist without charge but charge cannot exist without mass.

In higher classes you will learn that electric charges produce electric field which is a physical field around the charged particles.

How do we define One Coulomb charge?

The charge attained by 6.25×10^{18} electrons together is termed as 1 Coulomb.

This means that if a body is having a charge of $+1C$ then it has deficiency of 6.25×10^{18} electrons and if a body is having a charge of $-1C$ then it has excess of 6.25×10^{18} electrons.

Quantization of charge

Charges always exist in multiples of the elementary charge. This property is called Quantization of charge. The formula thus derived from this property is -

$$q = ne$$

where:

q = Total charge

n = number of electrons

e = elementary charge or charge on one electron

Potential difference

- Electric current is generated by the flow of charge but what makes the charge flow in the conductor? In order to understand this let's take the example of flow of water from the water storage tank at your house. The tank is preferably kept at the maximum height in the house so that a pressure difference can be created which will allow for the flow of water from high pressure to low.
This means a difference in water pressure is required for the flow of water. Similarly a difference in electric pressure is also required in a conductor for the flow of charges. This difference in electric pressure is known as Potential difference.

- When a conductor is not connected to any battery then the electrons in it continue to move in random direction. When a battery or a cell is connected to the conductor then the electrons experience a force which aligns them to flow unidirectionally from the negative terminal of the battery to the positive terminal.

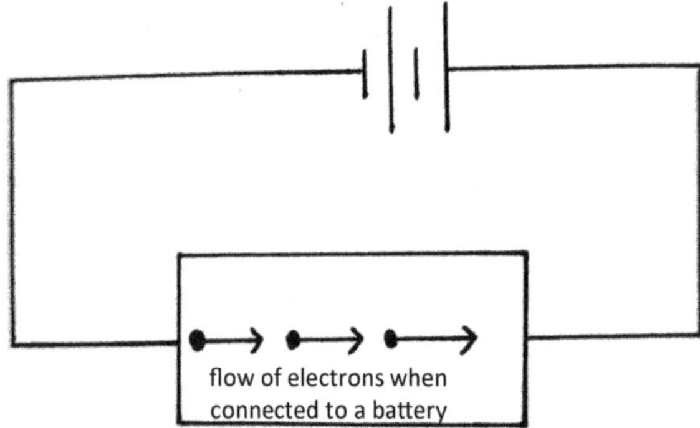

- The SI unit of Potential Difference is **volt or joule/coulomb**
where 1 volt = 1 joule/coulomb.

Potential difference is also expressed in the form of work done.

Some work needs to be done on a unit charge in order to move it from one point of the conductor to another and this work is called Potential difference.

If V denotes Potential difference, W denotes work done and q denotes charge then

$$V = \frac{W}{q}$$

- Potential difference across a conductor can be measured with the help of a device called Voltmeter. Potential difference can be created across the conductor with the help of cell or battery.

How can we define 1 volt potential difference?

In the given formula $V = \dfrac{W}{q}$,

If we substitute W = 1 Joule and q = 1 C, then V = 1 volt.
This can also be expressed in words.
If 1 joule work is done in moving 1 coulomb charge from one point of the conductor to another then the potential difference thus created is 1 volt.

Electric current

- When the charges present in the conductor starts to flow unidirectionally then it gives birth to electric current. If we want the charges in the body to flow unidirectionally then we need to connect a device which first creates potential difference. This device is preferably a cell or a battery.
  Thus current will be generated only if we are able to create potential difference.

- Electric current is defined as rate of flow of charges. It's SI unit is Ampere (A). The formula of current is :

$$I = \frac{q}{T}$$

where I denotes current, q denotes charge and T denotes time.

- Current is also expressed in coulomb/sec. Also, $1A = 1$ coulomb/sec. Smaller unit of current includes milliampere and microampere where **$1A = 10^3$ milliampere and $1 A = 10^6$ microampere.**

- Ammeter is a device which is used to measure the amount of current flowing in the circuit.

Ohm's Law

- A law can be defined as a set of rules which defines a behavioural pattern by establishing connection between its components. In simple terms law establishes connection between its components so in order to understand any law we need to first understand its components.
- Ohm's law establishes relationship between Potential difference and current flowing in a conductor.
- In Physics there are two kinds of basic relationship – Directly proportional and Inversely proportional. When two components are directly proportional then with the increase/decrease in the first component the second component will also increase/decrease. At the same time when two components are inversely proportional then with the increase/decrease in the first component, the second component will decrease/increase.
- Now before stating the exact law let's understand two points:
  a. In Ohm's law Potential difference and Current are in relationship.
  b. Both the components are directly proportional.
  Now let's understand the exact law:

- Ohm's Law states that the current flowing in the conductor is directly proportional to the potential difference across the ends of the conductor provided the physical condition and temperature of the conductor remains constant. This means that if we increase the potential difference across the ends of the conductor then the value of current flowing in it will also increase and vice versa. We will later understand why the temperature of the conductor should remain constant.

As per the above law,

$$V \alpha I$$

By removing the sign of proportionality and introducing a constant the above relationship becomes:

$$V = I.R$$

In the above expression R is a constant and is termed as ***Resistance.***

Graph of Ohm's Law

- A V-I graph is drawn for Ohm's law. The value of Potential difference (V) is represented on Y axis while the value of current (I) is represented on X axis.
- The slope of V-I graph gives us Resistance. Greater the slope, greater will be the Resistance.
- If we make a graph by plotting the value of Potential difference on X axis and Current on Y axis then the slope of such graph will give the value of $\frac{1}{R}$. This value is reciprocal of Resistance and is called Conductance.
- The resistors which follow Ohm's law are called Ohmic Resistors while those which do not follow Ohm's law are called Non Ohmic Resistors.
- The graphs are as follows:

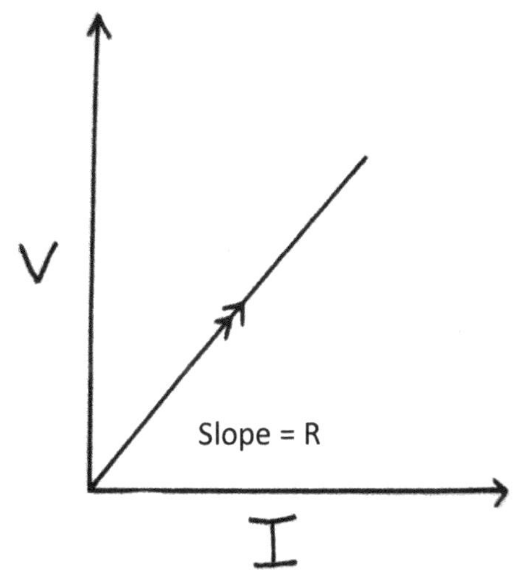

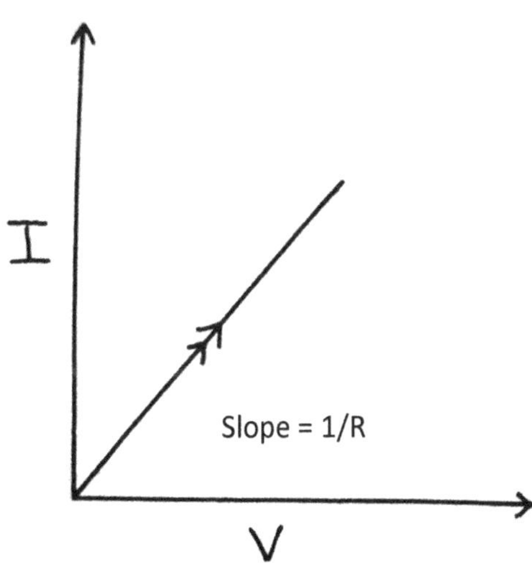

Experimental verification of Ohm's Law

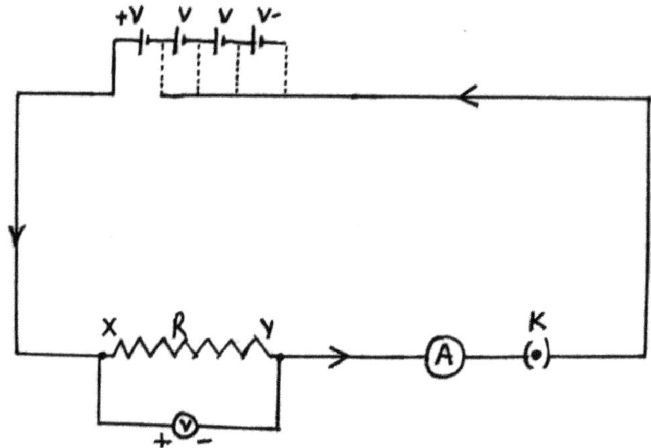

- In the above setup, first connect one cell in the circuit and note down the value of current in the circuit.
- Note this value of potential difference as V_1 and current as I_1.
- Now connect two cells in the circuit and note down the value of potential difference as V_2 and current as I_2.
- Repeat this step few more times and make an observation table of the data as shown below.

Potential difference (V)	V_1	V_2	V_3	V_4	V_5
Current (I)	I_1	I_2	I_3	I_4	I_5

- Plot a V-I graph from the given values.
- You will find a straight line graph which indicates that Ohm's law is being followed.

Numerical verification of Ohm's Law

- Let's take a resistor of 5 Ω and connect a battery of 5 volt in the circuit. The ammeter will measure the amount of current.
- The value of current can be derived from the formula $V = I.R$

- If V=I.R; then $I = \dfrac{V}{R}$.

- Substitute V = 5 volt and R = 5 Ω

- Then $I = \dfrac{5}{5} = 1$ A.

- Now increase the value of V to 10v, 15v, 20v and 25v and then subsequently calculate the value of I every time.

- If V = 10v then $I = \dfrac{10}{5} = 2$ A.

- If V = 15v then $I = \dfrac{15}{5} = 3$ A.

- If V = 20v then $I = \dfrac{20}{5} = 4$ A.

- If V = 25v then $I = \dfrac{25}{5} = 5$ A.

- The V-I table of the above data is as follows:

V	5v	10v	15v	20v	25v
I	1A	2A	3A	4A	5A

- Here we can see that with *equal increase in the value of Potential difference there is equal increase in the value of current* keeping the value of resistance constant.
This clearly proves Ohm's law.

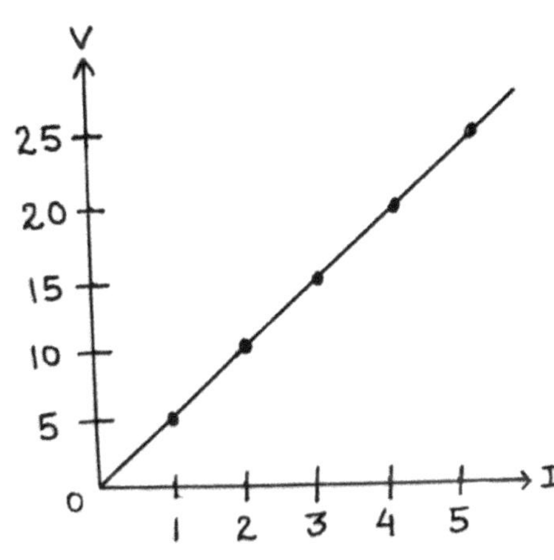

Concept of Resistance

- From the expression of Ohm's law we get a constant which is termed as Resistance.
- Resistance is defined as the obstruction or hindrance in the path of current.
- Let's try to understand the reason behind this obstruction provided to the current inside the conductor. When a potential difference is provided to the conductor then flow of charges takes place unidirectionally. But this flow is not ideal. There are *internal collisions* at the microscopic level which eventually leads to obstruction in the flow of current.
- The flow of charges also get hindered by *the attraction of the atoms* among which they move.
- The concept of Resistance can be remembered with the below flowchart:

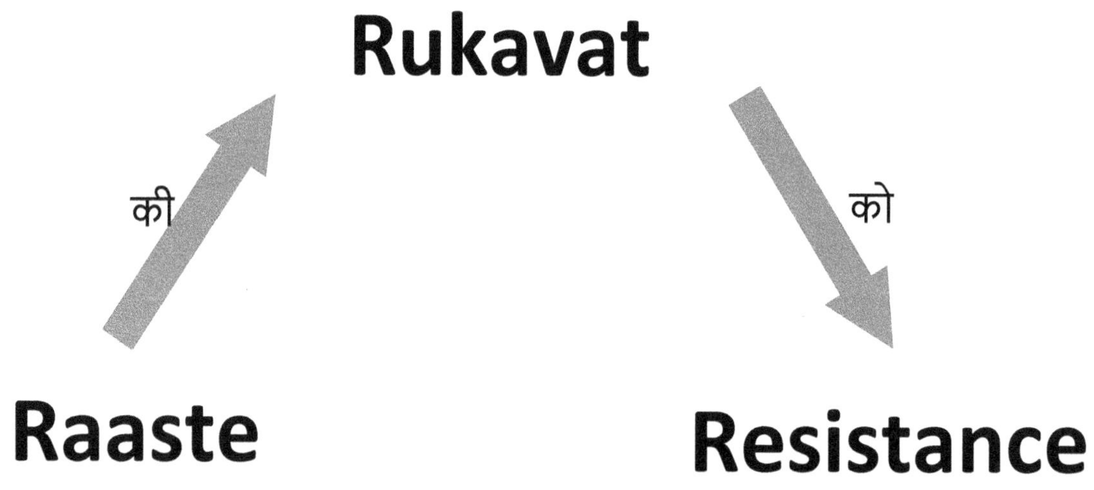

रास्ते की रुकावट को रेजिस्टेंस कहते हैं

Translation: The obstruction in the
path (of current) is known as
Resistance.

So remember the RRR formula to remember the concept of resistance.

Factors affecting Resistance:

The value of resistance can be changed by changing some constraints which are as following-

1 Length of conductor: $R \propto L$

Resistance is directly proportional to the length of the conductor.
As already stated that resistance is due to collisions at microscopic level so when the passage is long the collisions also increases.

2 Area of cross-section of conductor: $R \propto \dfrac{1}{A}$

Resistance is inversely proportional to the area of cross section. With increase in the value of area of cross section of conductor there is decrease in the value of Resistance and vice versa. This is because with increase in the area of cross section there are fewer internal collisions which decreases the obstruction.

3 Property of material (Resistivity):

Different types of material responds in different way to the flow of current. Some materials oppose the flow of current while some supports it. So Resistivity is an inherent property of every material which describes how strongly it opposes current.
If you carefully look at the previous two factors then we can combine the two expression together.

$R \propto L$ and

$R \propto \dfrac{1}{A}$

therefore, $R \propto \dfrac{L}{A}$

In order to remove the sign of proportionality we need to introduce a constant in the expression. That constant is rho (ρ). So now the expression becomes-

$$R = \rho . \dfrac{L}{A}$$

The SI unit of resistivity is $\Omega.\text{m}$.
Conductors tends to have less value of resistivity while Insulators tends to have more value of resistivity. *Resistivity varies with variation in temperature and material.*

4 Temperature:

With increase in the temperature of the conductor, there is increase in the internal collisions at microscopic level which increases the resistance.

Question: Now after studying ohm's law and also the factors affecting resistance can you answer why temperature of the conductor should remain constant in order to follow Ohm's law?

Answer: From the expression of Ohm's law ($V = I.R$) we get to know that ***Resistance is constant*** which we get from this equation. This means that current flowing in a conductor is directly proportional to the potential difference across its ends provided the resistance is constant.

Ohm's law will be followed when the value of resistance is constant but ***if we change the temperature then resistance will also change*** and the condition for Ohm's law will not be fulfilled.

Electric Circuit and its components

- An electric circuit is a continuous and complete path for the flow of charges. If we imagine charge or current as racing cars then the electric circuit can be imagined as their track.

- An electric circuit with an incomplete or broken path is called an **Open circuit.** The break in the circuit can be intentional(using a switch) or unintentional (like any fault in any equipment).

- An electric circuit with a complete and continuos path is called a **Closed circuit.**

- An electric circuit consists of several components which are shown in the below diagram:

Sl. No	Components	Symbols
1	An electic cell	
2	An battery or a combination of cells	
3	Plug key or switch (open)	
4	Plug key or switch (closed)	
5	A wire joint	
6	Wires crossing without joining	
7	Electric bulb	
8	A resistor of resistance R	
9	Variable resistance or rheostat	
10	Ammeter	
11	Voltmeter	

Combination of Resistance

- A resistor is a simple conducting material with a specific value of resistance.
- Two or more resistors can be added together in Series connection or Parallel connection.
- If multiple resistors are added together then their resistance can be altogether assumed as a single entity which is termed as Equivalent or Net Resistance. There are different formulae for Net resistance in series and parallel connections.

Series connection:

- If multiple resistors are connected in such a way that they provide only a single path for the flow of current then such type of connection is termed as Series connection.
- In series connection the current flowing in all the resistors is same.
- The potential difference across every resistor in a series connection will be different and the sum of the individual potential differences will be equal to the total potential difference in the circuit.

  $V = V_1 + V_2 + V_3$

- Let's try to understand how we can calculate Net resistance in a circuit having three resistors connected in series. In the diagram below you can see that the resistors R_1, R_2 and R_3 are connected in series.

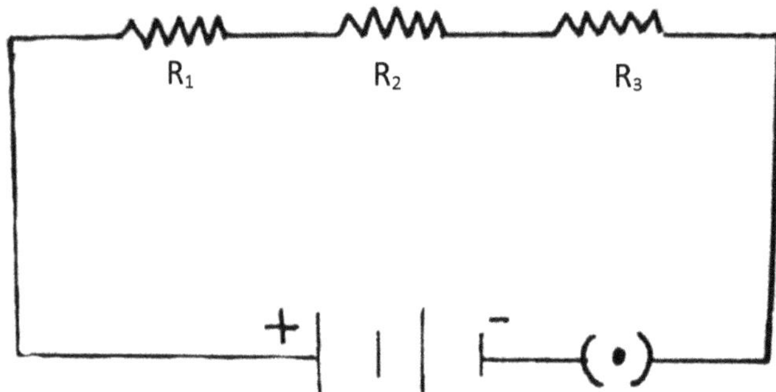

Since all the resistors are in series,
sum of the individual potential differences will be equal to the total potential difference in the circuit.

$V = V_1 + V_2 + V_3$ ------------------(i)

Applying Ohm's law in equation (i),
$V = I.R$,
$V_1 = I.R_1$,
$V_2 = I.R_2$,
$V_3 = I. R_3$
(Note that the value of current (I) remains the same because in series connection the current remains the same)

Now substitute the value of V, V_1, V_2 and V_3 in equation (i)
$I.R = I.R_1 + I.R_2 + I.R_3$
Taking the value of I common in all terms we get,
$I.R = I. (R_1 + R_2 + R_3)$
cancelling I from both the sides we get,

$$R = R_1 + R_2 + R_3$$

This is the formula to calculate Net resistance when resistors are connected in series.
Note: An Ammeter is always connected in series in the circuit

Parallel connection

- If multiple resistors are connected in such a way that they provide multiple path for the flow of current then such type of connection is termed as Parallel connection.
- In Parallel connection the Potential difference across all the resistors is same.
- The current flowing in every resistor will split into multiple parts and the sum of the individual current will be equal to the total current in the circuit.
$$I = I_1 + I_2 + I_3$$
- Let's try to understand how we can calculate Net resistance in a circuit having three resistors connected in parallel. In the diagram below you can see that the resistors R_1, R_2 and R_3 are connected in parallel.

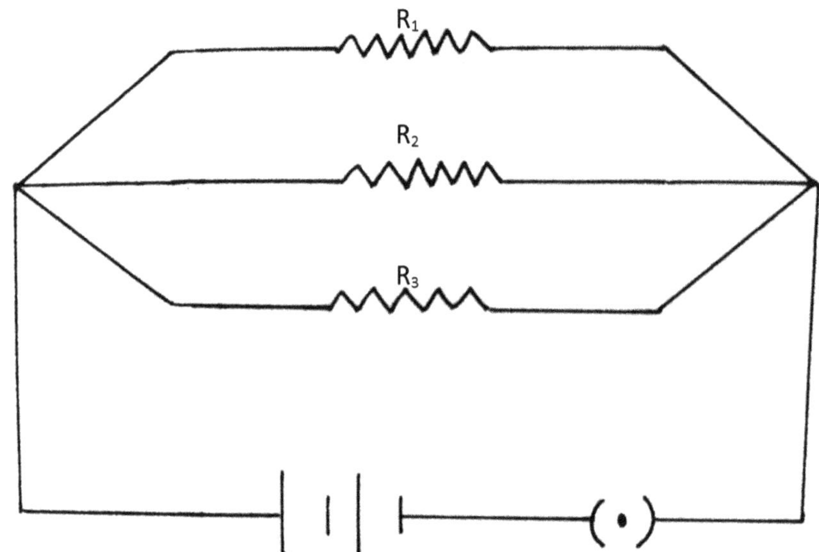

Since all the resistors are in parallel,
sum of the individual current will be equal to the total current in the circuit
$$I = I_1 + I_2 + I_3 \qquad \text{--------------------(i)}$$

Applying Ohm's law in equation (i),
$V = I.R$, so
$$I = \frac{V}{R}$$

$$I_1 = \frac{V}{R1},$$

$$I_2 = \frac{V}{R2},$$

$$I_3 = \frac{V}{R3},$$

(Note that the value of Potential difference (V) remains the same because in parallel connection the potential difference remains the same)

Now substitute the value of I, I_1, I_2 and I_3 in equation (i)

$$\frac{V}{R} = \frac{V}{R1} + \frac{V}{R2} + \frac{V}{R3}$$

Taking the value of V common in all terms we get,

$$V.\frac{1}{R} = V(\frac{1}{R1} + \frac{1}{R2} + \frac{1}{R3})$$

cancelling V from both the sides we get,

$$\frac{1}{R} = \frac{1}{R1} + \frac{1}{R2} + \frac{1}{R3}$$

This is the formula to calculate Net resistance when resistors are connected in Parallel.

Difference between Series and Parallel connection:

Series connection	Parallel connection
Multiple appliances can be controlled using a single switch in Series connection	Multiple appliances cannot be controlled using a single switch in Parallel connection
Series connection is cost effective since they require less wiring and switches.	Parallel connection is not cost effective since they require more wiring and switches.
If one appliance fails then the circuit will break and the current will not be able to reach the next appliance.	If one appliance fails then the circuit will not break and the current will still be able to reach the next appliance.
Appliances which require different values of current can not be connected in series since this type of connection provides only one value of current. For example a bulb and a heater requires different values of current for operation and that is why they should not be connected in series.	Appliances which require different values of current can be connected in parallel since this type of connection provides different value of current. For example a bulb and a heater requires different values of current for operation and that is why they should be connected in parallel.
The net resistance in case of series connection is greater than the individual resistance. For example if 4 resistors of 2Ω each are connected in series then the net resistance will be 8Ω.	The net resistance in case of parallel connection is lesser than the individual resistance. For example if 4 resistors of 2Ω each are connected in parallel the net resistance will be 0.5Ω.

Important points regarding Ammeter and Voltmeter:

- An ammeter is always connected in series with the circuit and a voltmeter is always connected in parallel with the circuit.
- An ammeter is a device with very low resistance so that it can measure maximum current in the circuit appropriately.
- A voltmeter is a device with high resistance so that it doesn't draw current through it.

Combination of Series and Parallel resistance

An electric circuit can have both series and parallel resistance. In such case the net resistance is calculated based on the type of connection at a particular place.

Example: In the diagram given below calculate the net resistance and the reading in the ammeter.

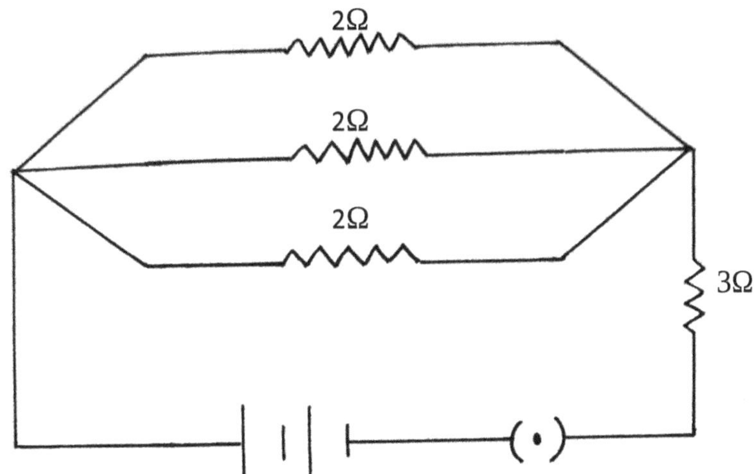

Solution: The resistors R_1, R_2 and R_3 are connected in parallel so we can calculate the net resistance and can replace them with a single resistance.

$$\frac{1}{R'} = \frac{1}{2} + \frac{1}{2} + \frac{1}{2}$$

$$\frac{1}{R'} = \frac{3}{2} \text{ and therefore } R' = \frac{2}{3}\Omega$$

The resistor R' is in series with the 3Ω resistor. So they will be added together to get the net resistance.

$$\text{Rnet} = \frac{2}{3}\Omega + 3\Omega$$

$$\text{Rnet} = 3.67\Omega$$

Heating effect of electric current

When an appliance is used some part of the current from the supply is consumed for the useful work while some part of the source energy gets dissipated in the form of heat. This is known as Heating effect of electric current. There are many devices like electric iron, electric heater etc. whose working is based on the heating effect of current.

Joule's Law of heating:
This law explains the factors affecting the heat produced in a resistor.
It states that the heat produced is directly proportional to:
a. square of the current for a given resistance
b. resistance for a given current
c. time for which the current flows into the resistor.

From the above law if,
H = Heat produced
I = current for a given resistance
R = resistance for a given current
T = time for which the current flows
then,
$H \alpha I^2$, $H \alpha R$ and $H \alpha T$
therefore,

$$H = I^2Rt$$

Example: How much amount of heat is produced in 5 seconds in a 10 Ω resistor if the potential difference is 20 v?

Answer:

$$I = \frac{V}{R}$$

$$I = \frac{20}{10} = 2\,A$$

$$H = I^2Rt$$

$$H = 2^2 \times 10 \times 5 = \textbf{200 joules.}$$

Some Practical applications of heating effect of current

1. Appliances like **Electric geyser, toaster, kettle, iron and oven** works on the heating effect of current.

2. An **Electric bulb** is also based on the heating effect of current. It consists of a filament which is generally made up of tungsten whose melting point is very high. The heating of this filament produces light in the electric bulb. The filament is enclosed within an insulated covering which protects it from getting oxidised. The filament inside the casing lasts longer because it is sealed with chemically inactive nitrogen and argon.

3. An **Electric fuse** is also based on this principle. It helps in stopping the flow of undesirably high amount of current. It is connected in series with the appliance. If a current larger than the specified value flows through the circuit then the temperature of the fuse wire increases which melts it and finally breaks the circuit preventing the appliance from the extra current.

It should always be noted that the rating of fuse wire must always be either equal to greater than the value of safe current. This means that if the maximum permissible current for a device is 10 ampere then a fuse of 10 ampere should be used. The rating of fuse wire is always in whole number so if the maximum permissible current for a device is 6.2 ampere then we must use a fuse of 7 ampere.

How to calculate the value of safe current/maximum permissible current?

The formula of Power is used to calculate the value of safe current.

$P = V.I$

Now if we make I the subject, the formula would become:

$$I = \frac{P}{V}$$

Here in the above formula 'I' indicates the value of maximum permissible/safe current.

Example: An electric geyser of 1500 watt is connected to a 220v supply. A fuse of what rating must be connected?

Solution:

$$I = \frac{P}{V} = \frac{1500}{220} = 6.81 \text{ A}$$

So, a fuse of 7A must be used.

The fuse wire specifically possess two basic property:

a. Low melting point   b. High resistivity/resistance

Note: *Other than the fuse wire, the heating element which is used in those devices which are based on heating effect of current possess **high melting point**. They also possess **high resistivity**.*

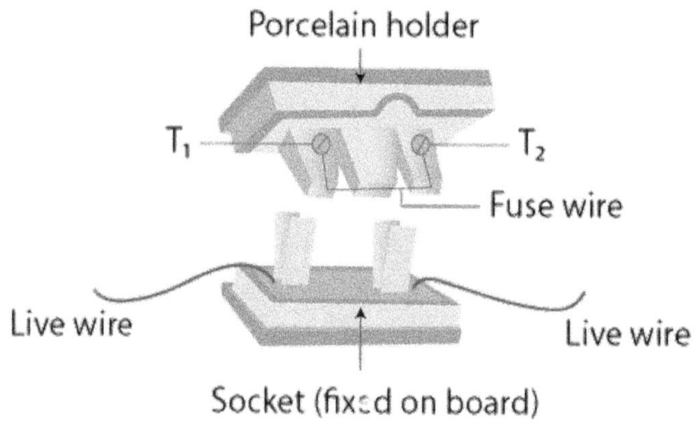

Disadvantages of heating effect of current:

1. The heat produced is sometime so much that it tends to damage the device.
2. The heat dissipated is sometimes a waste of energy.
3. Some appliance have an in built arrangements for cooling of equipments. Either they have air passage or they have small add ons like fans which prevents any kind of malfunction.

Think before answer: Now can you answer why the ATM machine chambers have ACs?

Electric Power

Definition: It is defined as the rate of consumption of electrical energy.
SI unit: watt

Formula: P $= \dfrac{E}{T}$

where P denotes Electric Power, E denotes Electrical energy and T denotes Time period.
Other unit: Joule/sec
Conversions: 1 watt = 1 joule/sec
        1 kilowatt = 1000 watt
        1 Megawatt = 10^6 watt
There is one more formula to calculate Power which is:

$$P = V.I$$

So from here we get one more unit of Power which is **Volt.Ampere.**
Remember that 1 watt = 1 volt.ampere

Electric Energy

From the formula of Power which is **P** $= \dfrac{E}{T}$ if we make E (electrical energy) the subject

the expression would be:

$$E = P.T$$

From the above expression,
we can define electrical energy as the ***Product of Power and time.***
An Electric meter is a device which is used to measure the amount of electrical energy
consumed. The commercial unit of electrical energy is kilowatt.hour (KWh).
1 Kilowatt hour is defined as the electrical energy consumed when 1 kilowatt of power is
consumed for one hour.
The electricity bill generated by the Electric meter is based on the total units of electrical
energy consumed in a specific period of time.

Billing system

The billing system helps us to determine the total amount of money which a consumer
needs to pay for a stipulated period of time. The rate of 1 unit of electrical energy is
defined by the government and with the help of this the total amount is calculated.
For example if the rate of electrical energy is ₹8/unit and a consumer gets a bill of 200
units then the billing amount will be: 8 x 200 = ₹1600
The formula to calculate the bill is:
Rate of one unit x Total units consumed

Example: An electrical appliance rated [220v, 0.2A] is used for 10 hours everyday. If the
rate of electrical energy is ₹10/unit then calculate the electricity bill for 30 days.

Solution:

$P = V.I$
$P = 220 \times 0.2 = 110$ watt *(After this step convert the value from watt to kilowatt)*
$P = 110$ watt $= 0.110$ kW
Electrical energy $= P \times T$
(make sure that time must be in hour)
$E = P \times T$
$E = 0.110 \times 10 = 1.1$ KWh *(This is the electrical energy consumed for one day)*
Electrical energy consumed in 30 days $= 1.1$ KWh $\times 30 =$ **33 KWh.**
Using unitary method:
If one unit costs ₹8 then
33 units will cost $=$ ₹8 $\times$ 33 units
Total bill = ₹264

Similarly if multiple appliances are used then the bill by individual appliances gets added
to calculate the total bill.

CHAPTER AT A GLANCE – NCERT BASED IMPORTANT POINTS

- Charge on 1 electron is 1.6×10^{-19} C
- The direction of current is taken opposite to the direction of flow of electrons.
- Potential difference is created by a cell or a battery.
- Resistance is the obstruction in the path of current.
- Ohm's law states that the current flowing in a circuit is directly proportional to the potential difference across its end.
- A voltmeter is connected in parallel and an ammeter is connected is series.
- Power is defined as the rate of electrical energy.
- A Fuse wire has low melting point and high resistivity.

Question 1: What does an electric circuit mean?

Answer 1: An electric circuit can be simply defined as a path for successful transmission of electric current. It consists of wires, a device the produce current and a device or few devices which use the current.

Question 2: Define the unit of current.

Answer 2: The unit of current is Ampere.

1 Ampere is defined as the current produced when a charge of 1 coulomb flows for 1 second across the conductor.

Question 3: Calculate the number of electrons constituting 1 coulomb of charge.

Answer 3: One electron possess 1.6 x 10^{19} C charge, therefore 1 coulomb of charge would

attain $\dfrac{1}{1.6\,x\,10^{19}C}$ = 6.25 x 10^{18} number of electrons.

Question 4: Name a device that helps to maintain a potential difference across a conductor.

Answer 4: Battery or cell is a device that helps to maintain potential difference across a conductor.

Question 5: What is meant by saying that the potential difference between two points is 1 V?

Answer 5: When 1 joule of work is done to move a charge of 1 coulomb from one end of the conductor to another in 1 seconds then the potential difference developed across the ends of the conductor is said to be 1 volt.

Question 6: How much energy is given to each coulomb of charge passing through a 6 V battery?

Answer 6: Since V = $\dfrac{W}{Q}$ therefore W = V.Q

In the question Q = 1 C and V = 6V so calculating W from this we get,

W = 1 x 6 = 6 J

Question 7: On what factors does the resistance of a conductor depends?

Answer 7: The resistance of a conductor depends on the following factors:

a. Resistance is directly proportional to length of the conductor.

b. Resistance is inversely proportional to the area of cross section of the conductor.

c. Resistance depends on the material of the conductor.

d. Resistance is directly proportional to the temperature of the conductor.

Question 8: Will current flow more easily through a thick wire or a thin wire of the same material when connected through a same source? Why ?

Answer 8: When connected to the same source current flow more easily through a thick wire than a thin wire of the same material since resistance is inversely proportional to the area of cross section of the conductor. As a result a thick wire would offer less resistance to the current than the thin wire.

Question 9: Let the resistance of an electrical component remains constant while the potential difference across the two ends of the component decreases to half of its former value. What change will occur in the current through it?

Answer 9: According to Ohm's law if the resistance is kept constant then current flowing through the conductor is directly proportional to the potential difference across its end. Therefore, if the potential difference is reduced to half then the value of current would also decrease by half of its former value.

Question 10: Why are coils of electric toasters and electric irons made of an alloy rather than a pure metal?

Answer 10: Alloys tends to have more resistivity and melting point as compared to pure metals and that is why coils of electric toasters and electric irons are made up of an alloy rather than a pure metal.

Question 11:

	Material	Resistivity (Ω.m)
Conductors	Silver	1.6×10^{-8}
	Copper	1.62×10^{-8}
	Aluminium	2.63×10^{-8}
	Tungsten	5.2×10^{-8}
	Nickel	6.84×10^{-8}
	Iron	10×10^{-8}
	Chromium	12.9×10^{-8}
	Mercury	94×10^{-8}
	Manganese	1.84×10^{-6}
Alloys	Constantan (alloy of Cu and Ni)	49×10^{-6}
	Manganin (alloy of Cu, Mn and Ni)	44×10^{-6}
	Nichrome (alloy of Ni, Cr, Mn and Fe)	100×10^{-6}
Insulators	Glass	$10^{10} - 10^{14}$
	Hard rubber	$10^{13} - 101^{6}$
	Ebonite	$10^{15} - 10^{17}$
	Diamond	$10^{12} - 10^{13}$
	Paper (dry)	10^{12}

Use the data in table above to answer the following:

a. Which among iron and mercury is a better conductor?
b. Which material is the best conductor?

Answer 11: a. Iron is a better conductor than mercury since its resistivity is lesser.
b. As per the data provided in the above table Silver is considered as the best conductor since its resistivity is minimum.

Question 12: Draw a schematic diagram of a circuit consisting of a battery of three cells of 2 volt each, a 5 Ω resistor, an 8 Ω resistor and a 12 Ω resistor and a plug key all connected in series.

Answer 12:

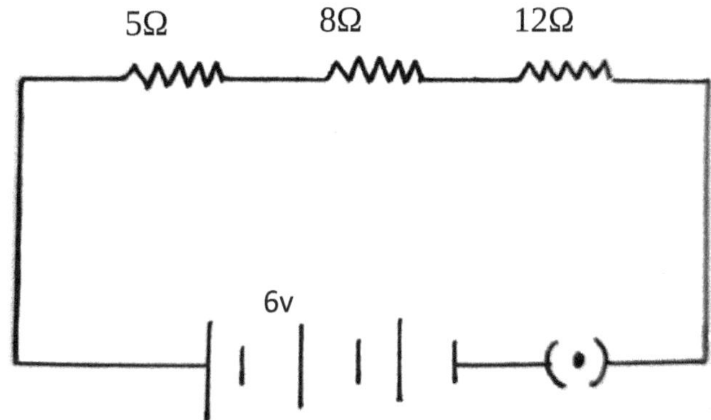

Question 13: Redraw the circuit of question 12, putting an ammeter to measure the current through the resistors and a voltmeter to measure the potential difference across the 12 Ω resistor. What would be the readings in the ammeter and the voltmeter?

Answer 13:

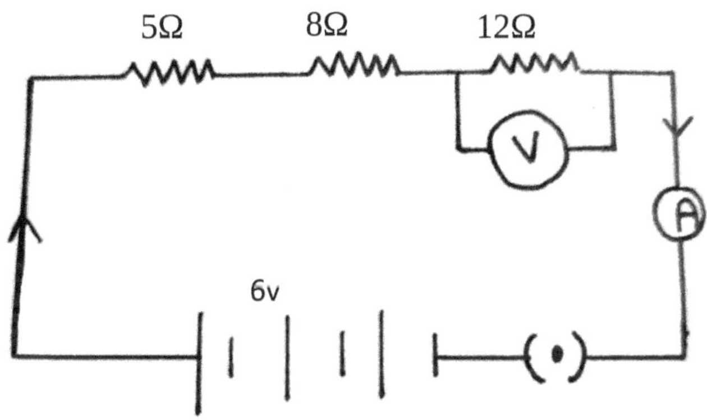

Net resistance of the circuit

R = 5+ 8+ 12 = 25 Ω

V = 6 V

$$I = \frac{V}{R} = \frac{6}{25} = 0.24 \text{ A}$$

Reading of the ammeter will be 0.24 A

Let the potential difference across the 12 ohm resistor is V'.

V' = I.R

V' = 0.24 x 12 = 2.88 V

Reading of the voltmeter will be 2.88 V.

Question 14: Judge the equivalent resistance when the following are connected in parallel–

a. 1 Ω and 10^6 Ω

b. 1 Ω and 10^3 Ω and 10^6 Ω

Answer 14:

a. When 1 Ω and 10^6 Ω are connected in parallel then the Net resistance will be R which can be calculated by using the formula of Parallel resistance

$$\frac{1}{R} = \frac{1}{1} + \frac{1}{10^6}$$

$$R = \frac{10^6}{10^6 + 1}$$

Since 10^6 is very close to $(10^6 + 1)$

we can say that that ratio is very close to 1.

Therefore, **R is equivalent to 1 Ω**

b. When a 1 Ω, 10^3 and 10^6 are connected tin parallel then the Net resistance can be calculated by using the formula of Parallel resistance

$$\frac{1}{R} = \frac{1}{1} + \frac{1}{10^3} + \frac{1}{10^6}$$

$$\frac{1}{R} = \frac{10^6 + 10^3 + 1}{10^6} = \frac{1000000}{1001001} = 0.999 \; \Omega$$

Question 15: An electric lamp of 100 Ω, a toaster of resistance 50 Ω and a water filter of resistance 500 Ω are connected in parallel to a 220v source. What is the resistance of an electric iron connected to the same source that takes as much current as all three appliances, and what is the current through it?

Answer 15: First calculate the net resistance of all the devices which will be equal to the resistance of the electric iron.

$$\frac{1}{R} = \frac{1}{100} + \frac{1}{50} + \frac{1}{500}$$

$$\mathbf{R} = \frac{500}{16}\mathbf{\Omega}$$

According to Ohm's law V = I.R

therefore $I = \dfrac{V}{R} = \dfrac{220 \times 16}{500} = \mathbf{7.04 \; A}$

Question 16: What are the advantages of connecting electrical devices in parallel with the battery instead of connecting wires in series?

Answer 16: The advantages of connecting electrical devices in parallel with the battery are as follows:

a. If one device fails the others won't get affected.

b. There is same voltage across each device

c. When devices are connected in parallel then the Net resistance in the circuit will decrease.

Question 17: How can three resistors of resistances 2 Ω, 3 Ω and 6 Ω be connected to give a total resistance of -

a. 4 Ω   b. 1 Ω?

Answer 17: In order to get the desired result we need to try multiple combinations.

a. Let's say R1 = 2 Ω, R2 = 3 Ω and R3 = 6 Ω

By connecting R2 and R3 in parallel we get:

$$\frac{1}{R} = \frac{1}{3} + \frac{1}{6}$$

R = 2Ω

Now by connecting R and R1 in series we get = 2Ω + 2Ω = **4Ω**

b. Connecting all the resisters in parallel we get:

$$\frac{1}{R} = \frac{1}{2} + \frac{1}{3} + \frac{1}{6}$$

R = 1Ω

Question 18: What is the highest and the lowest total resistance that can be secured by combination of four coils of resistance 4 Ω, 8 Ω, 12 Ω and 24 Ω?

Answer 18: The highest total resistance can be secured by connecting all the resistors in series.

R = 4Ω + 8Ω + 12Ω + 24Ω = **48Ω**

The lowest total resistance can be secured by connecting all the resistors in parallel.

$$\frac{1}{R} = \frac{1}{4} + \frac{1}{8} + \frac{1}{12} + \frac{1}{24}$$

R = 2Ω

Question 19: Why does the cord of an electrical heater not glow while the heating element does?

Answer 19: The heating element offers very high resistance to the flow of current as compared to the electrical heater. As a result of this when current passes through the heating element it produces a large amount of heat due to which it starts glowing and at the same time when current passes through the cord of an electrical heater the resistance offered is less due to which it only gets warm and does not glow.

Question 20: Compute the heat generated while transferring 96000 c of charge in one hour through a potential difference of 50 v.

Answer 20:

Q = 96000 C

t = 1hr = 60 x 60 = 3600 s

V = 50 v

We know that $I = \dfrac{Q}{t} = \dfrac{96000}{3600} = \dfrac{80}{3} A$

Let the heat generated be H = V x I x t

$H = 50 \times \dfrac{80}{3} \times 3600$

$H = 4.8 \times 10^6 \, J$

Question 21: An electric iron of resistance 20 Ω takes a current of 5 A. Calculate the heat developed in 30 s.

Answer 21: $H = I^2 \times R \times t$

$H = 5^2 \times 20 \times 30$

$H = 15000 \, J$

Question 22: What determines the rate at which energy is delivered by a current?

Answer 22: The rate at which energy is delivered by a current is termed as **Electric Power**.

Question 23: An electric motor takes 5 A from a 220 V line. Determine the power of the motor and the energy consumed in 2 hour.

Answer 23: P = Vx I

P = 220 x 5 = 1100 watt or 1.100 kilowatt

Energy = Power x time

(note that in this formula Power must be in kilowatt and time must be in hour)

Energy = 1.1 x 2 = 2.2 KwH

The answer can also be calculated in Joules. In this case Power will be in watt and time will be in seconds.

Energy = 1100 x (2 x 3600) = 7920000 J

Magnetic effects of electric current

Chapter: Magnetic effect of current

Introduction

There are several kinds of effects produced by the current. If we take the example of appliances like electric geyser then it works on the heating effect of current. At the same time if we talk about the electrolysis of water then it is based on the chemical effects of current.

If we pass electric current through a conductor then it develops a magnetic field around it. This effect is commonly termed as the magnetic effect of current which we will be studying in detail in this chapter.

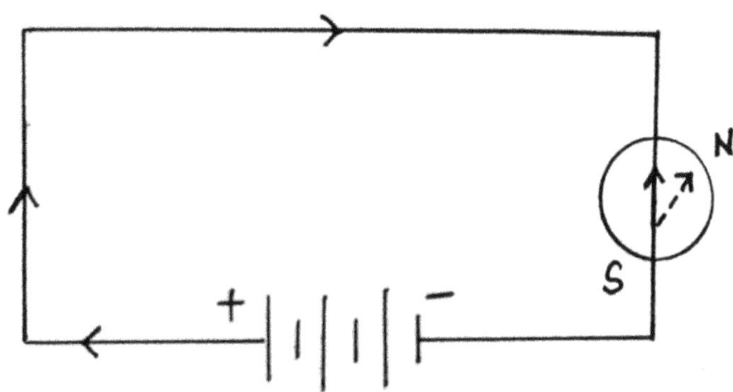

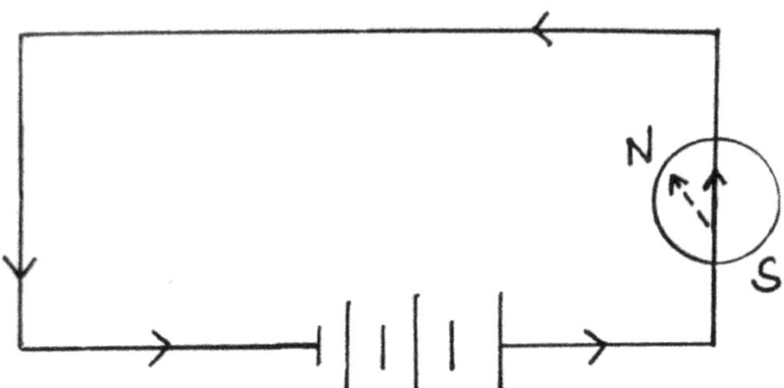

Note: *In the above two diagrams we can see that the direction of deflection in the compass is reversed by reversing the direction of current.*

Oersted Experiment

Hans Christian Oersted performed a simple experiment which proved that current and magnetism are linked together.
In this experiment he used a battery, platinum wire and a magnetic compass.
The *diagram* below shows how the set up was created.

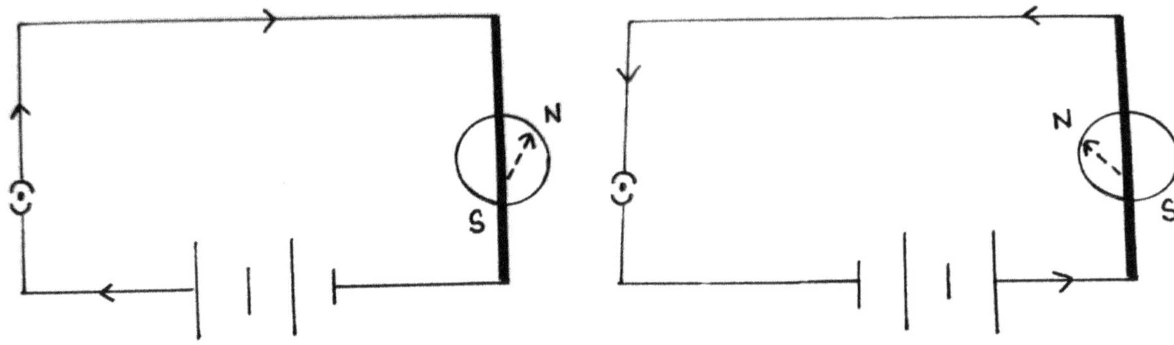

- The first observation was noted that there was no deflection in the magnetic compass when the key was in the off position.
- The second observation was noted that there was some deflection in the magnetic compass when the key was pressed on.
- He also noted that by reversing the direction of current, the direction of deflection in the compass also got reversed.

This experiment proved that there exists a magnetic field around a current carrying conductor whose direction changes with the direction of current.

Magnetic field and Magnetic field lines

Magnetic field is defined as the area around a magnet where it's properties can be sensed. It extends up to a certain level around the magnet depending on it's size and power. A powerful magnet tends to have a larger magnetic field as compared to a weaker magnet. Magnetic field is a vector quantity. The unit of magnetic field strength is 'Oersted' in the honor of Sir Hans Oersted who discovered the link between current and magnetic field. The magnetic field in a given region is represented by Magnetic field lines.
These lines are abstract in nature and helps us to visualize the magnetic field.

Properties of magnetic field lines:

- Outside a magnet the magnetic field lines emerge from the North pole and merge at the south pole.
- Inside a magnet the magnetic field lines move from South to North pole.
- The field lines are closed curves.
- The direction of field lines at a particular point on the line can be determined by making a tangent at that point.
- The degree of closeness of the lines determines the strength of the field.
- Two magnetic field lines never intersect each other. If we assume two lines to be intersecting at a point then it means that there would be two directions of the field at a point which is technically impossible.

Why does a magnetic compass shows deflection when it is brought in a magnetic field?

The needle of the magnetic compass is a small bar magnet. The ends of the needle are directed towards the North-South pole. The end seeking towards the North is called the North pole and the end seeking towards the South is called South pole.
When current is passed through a conductor it acquires a magnetic field or in other words we can say that it acts like a magnet. The field lines of this magnet and the needle of the compass which is also a small magnet interacts with each other and since the like poles repel and unlike poles attracts, it becomes the reason for deflection in the magnetic compass.

How can we obtain the magnetic field lines around a bar magnet?

We can obtain the magnetic field lines around a bar magnet with the help of very simple experiment. For that we require a bar magnet, a white sheet of paper and a wooden board.

- Place the white sheet of paper on the wooden board.
- At the centre of the paper gently place a bar magnet
- Now place the compass near the North pole of the magnet. You would notice that the South pole of the compass points towards the North pole of the magnet. At the same time the North pole of the compass points away from the North pole of the magnet.
- Mark the positions of the North and South pole of the compass.
- Now change the position of the compass in such a way that the South pole of the compass occupies the position which was previously occupied by the North pole of the compass and then mark the positions of both the poles again.
- Repeat this process till you reach the South pole of the magnet.
- Join all the points together on the white sheet and form a smooth curve.
- The line thus formed is the Magnetic field line.
- Draw as many lines possible.

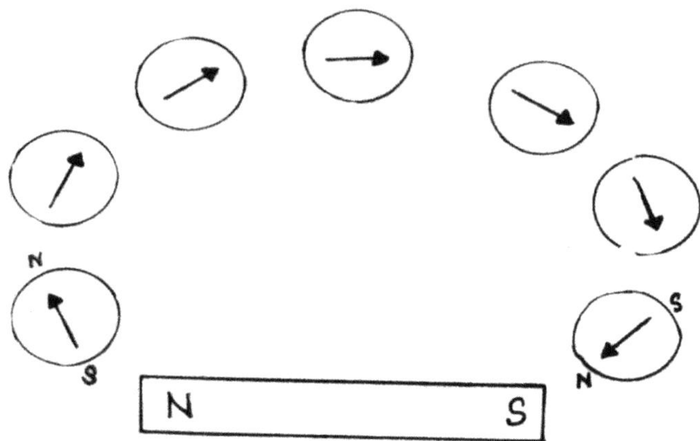

We can also perform one more activity to get the magnetic field lines around a bar magnet. For that we require a wooden board, a bar magnet, a white sheet of paper and some iron fillings. Follow these steps:

- Place a white sheet of paper on a wooden board.
- Now gently place a bar magnet at the centre of the paper.
- Slowly sprinkle the iron fillings around the bar magnet.
- Make sure you sprinkle the fillings evenly at all the places.
- After sprinkling the iron fillings gently tap the paper few times.
- You would notice that the fillings arrange themselves in a given pattern.
- The lines of the iron fillings denotes the magnetic field lines.

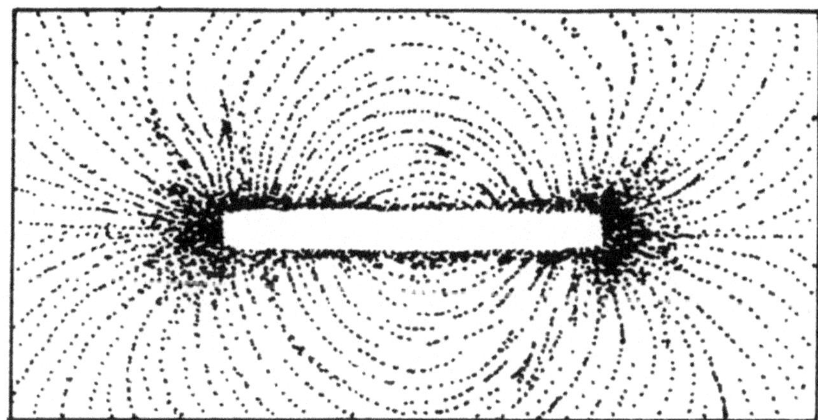

In this chapter we will be studying about the magnetic field and field lines around several components which include a bar magnet, a straight current carrying conductor, a circular loop and a solenoid. So let's start!

Magnetic field around a bar magnet

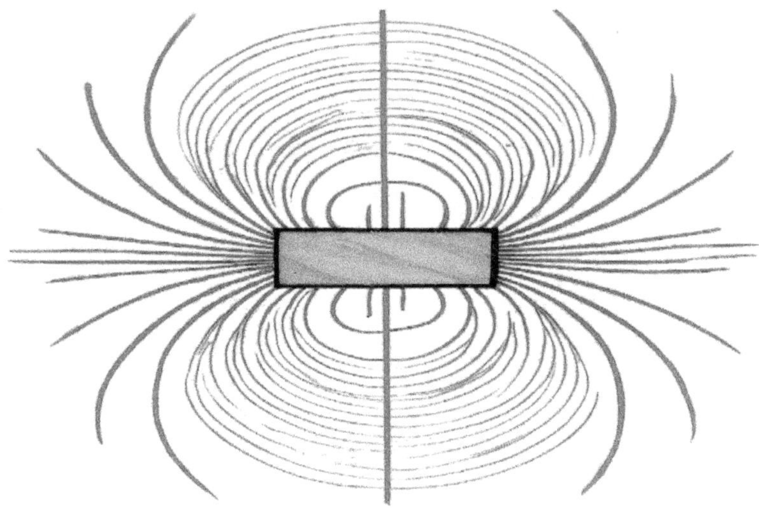

- The field lines are closed curves around the bar magnet.
- Outside the magnet the field lines emerge from the North pole and goes towards the south pole. Inside the magnet these lines move from the South pole to the North pole.
- The magnetic field strength around a bar magnet is maximum at the pole and that is why the density of field lines is also maximum near the poles.
- The magnetic field strength inside the bar magnet is uniform and therefore the field lines are parallel in nature. Remember, parallel field lines indicates uniform magnetic field.
- As we move away from the bar magnet the magnetic field tends to become weaker and therefore the density of the field lines also decrease.

Magnetic field around a straight current carrying conductors

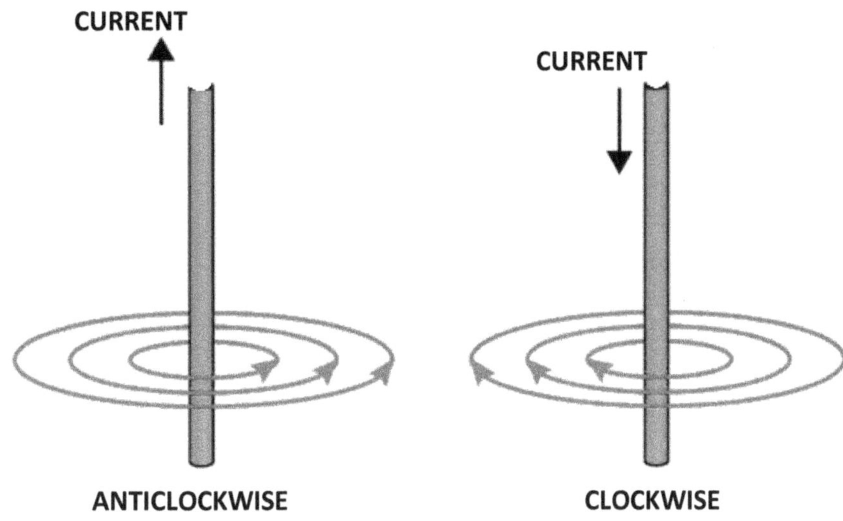

- The magnetic field lines around a straight current carrying conductor is in the shape of concentric circles.
- The strength of the magnetic field is maximum at the centre of the concentric circle. The strength decreases as we move away from the centre.
- The direction of the field lines is given by Right hand thumb rule.
- The direction of the field lines can be reversed by reversing the direction of the current in the conductor.
- The concentric circles tends to become larger and larger as we move away from the conductor.

Right hand thumb rule

A straight current carrying conductor produces a magnetic field around it and we have also studied that the field lines are in the shape of concentric circles. But apart from this we also need to find out the direction of field lines. Since the lines are circular in shape so it is pretty much evident that the direction will be either clockwise or anticlockwise.
With the help of Right hand thumb rule we determine the direction of magnetic field lines.
In order to find out the direction of field lines we assume that we hold the conductor with our right hand in such a way that our Thumb indicates the direction of flow of current and direction of curls of our finger indicates the direction of magnetic field lines.
This is the Right Hand Thumb rule.

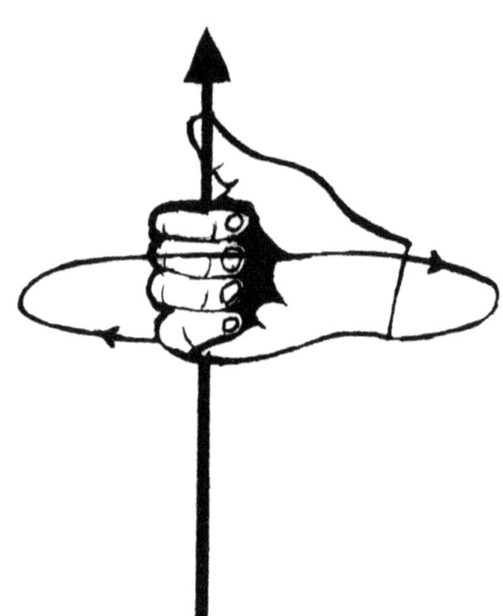

Question: Current in a wire flows horizontally from West to the East direction. Find out the direction of magnetic field produced around the wire.

Solution: Imagine a wire right in front of your eyes in which the current is flowing from West to the East direction. Align your right hand in such a way that you are holding the wire and your thumb is in the direction of flow of current.
Now if you look from the West end the field lines will be in anticlockwise direction and if you look from the East end the field lines will be in clockwise direction.

Trick to find the direction of magnetic field lines

There's one trick which can help you in finding the direction of magnetic field lines
around a straight current carrying conductor.
If the current is moving in the upward or in the downward direction in the conductor then
all you need to do is just to remember this acronym: AU or CD
When we say AU then,
A means anticlockwise and U means upward

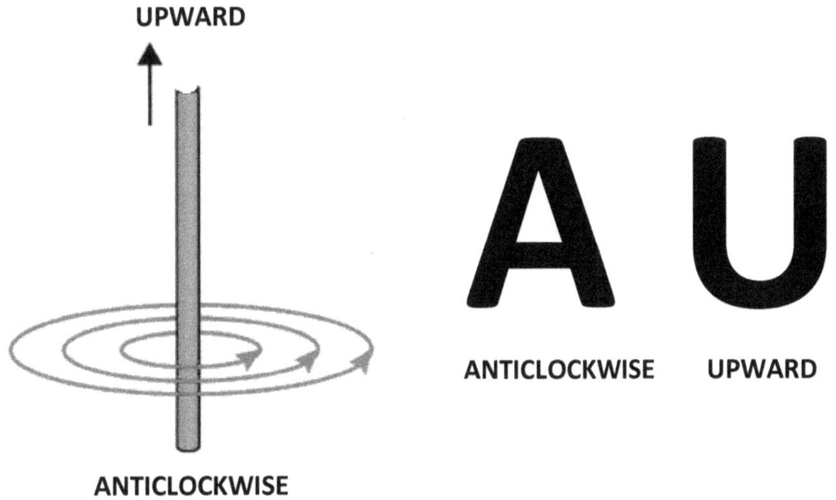

When we say CD then,
C means clockwise and D means downward

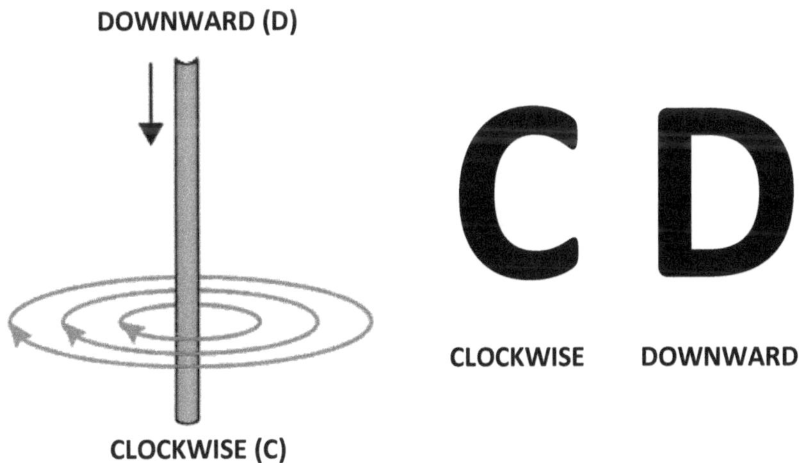

So with this help of this trick you can remember the direction of magnetic field lines
around a current carrying conductor.

Magnetic field around a current carrying circular loop

If we bend the straight current carrying conductor it will form a circular loop. Now we need to find out the nature and direction of magnetic field produced around the loop. Take a cardboard and insert the wire from downward to vertically upward direction. Bend the wire and then again insert it back into the cardboard. Now if you look at the wire it would look like a circular loop of wire carrying current. Once the current is supplied the wire forms a magnetic field around it.

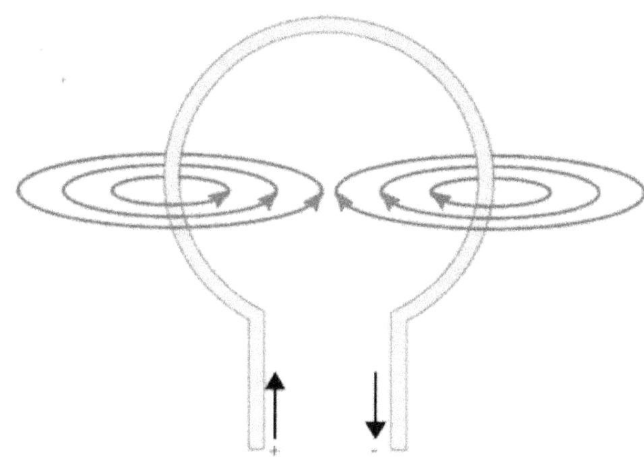

- The density of magnetic field lines will be more near the wire but as we move away from the wire, the density would decrease and the curves will become bigger in size.
- When we reach the centre of the circular loop then the magnetic field lines are almost straight lines.
- The direction of magnetic field lines at any section of the loop can be determined with the help of right had thumb rule.
- By increasing the value of current we can increase the strength of magnetic field around the loop.
- If we increase the number of loop carrying the same current in the same direction then the strength of the magnetic field would also increase.

Magnetic field due to a current in a Solenoid

When an insulated conductor wire is highly coiled in the form of circular turns and is wrapped together in the form of a cylinder then it is called a Solenoid.

The pattern of magnetic field lines around a solenoid is given below in the diagram.

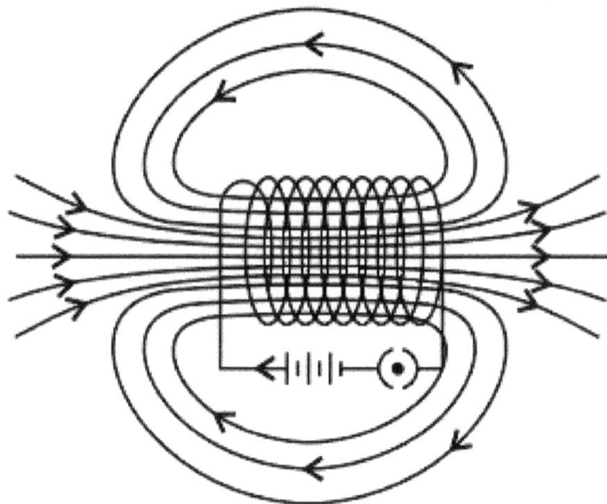

- The pattern of magnetic field lines around a current carrying solenoid matches with that around a bar magnet.
- One end of the solenoid behaves as the North pole while the other behaves as a South pole.

> **Note:** *In order to remember that which end of the solenoid will behave as the North and which will behave as South pole just remember this short and simple trick-*
>
> *N stands for North and N stands for Negative. This means that the end of the solenoid which connects with the negative terminal of the battery will behave as the North pole while the other end will behave as the South pole.*

- The magnetic field lines inside the solenoid will be parallel. These parallel lines indicates that the magnetic field inside the solenoid will be uniform i.e. same throughout at all the points.
- The North-South polarity attained by the solenoid can be reversed by reversing the polarity of the battery.
- The magnetic field strength of the solenoid can be increased by increasing the number of turns in the solenoid. If we insert a soft iron core inside the solenoid then it will get magnetised due to the strong magnetic field. The magnet which is formed in this way will be termed as Electromagnet.

Force due to magnetic field

A current carrying conductor develops a magnetic field around it.
When this current carrying conductor is placed in a magnetic field then the two magnetic fields interact with each other and as a result produces a force which is experienced by the current carrying conductor.

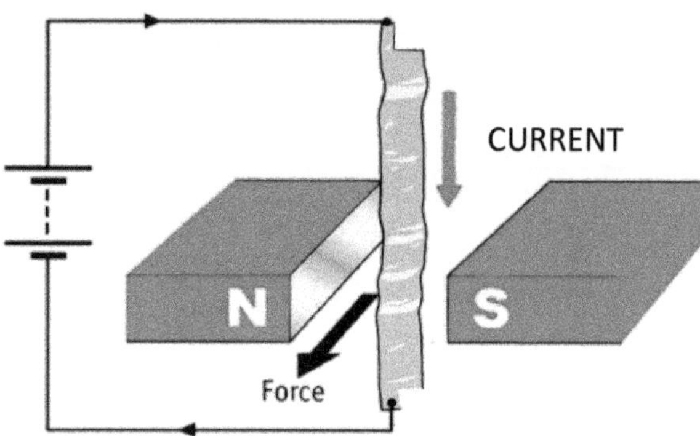

Factors affecting the force on the current carrying conductor:

1. Strength of the magnetic field:
If the current carrying conductor is placed in a weak magnetic field then the force experienced by it will also be weak and if the conductor is placed in a strong magnetic field then it will experience a strong force.

2. Strength of the current in the conductor:
The force experienced by the conductor is directly proportional to the current flowing in the conductor.

3. Length of the conductor:
The force experienced by the conductor is directly proportional to the length of the conductor. This means that a long current carrying conductor will experience more force as compared to a short conductor.

4. Angle between the conductor and the magnet:
When the direction of current is parallel to the direction of magnetic field then the force experienced is minimum and when the direction of current is perpendicular to the direction of magnetic field then the force experienced by the conductor is maximum.

Fleming's Left hand rule

We have already studied that when a current carrying conductor is placed in a magnetic field then it experience a force. The direction of this force can be determined with the help of a simple rule called Fleming's left hand rule.

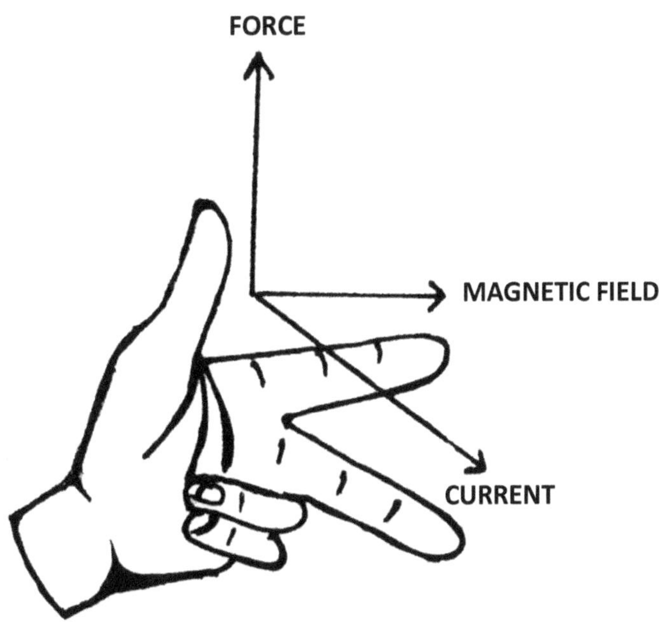

In this rule we take the help of our left hand and stretch the thumb, forefinger and middle finger in such a way that all three are mutually perpendicular to each other just like it is shown in the above diagram.
If we assume that the direction of the forefinger is in the direction of magnetic field and the direction of middle finger is in the direction of current then the direction of thumb would give the direction of force acting on the conductor.

Applications of force acting on current carrying conductors

- Electric motor
- Electric generator
- Loudspeaker etc.

Domestic Electric Circuits

- The electric cables with which electricity is supplied at our homes consists of three wires. The red coloured wire is known as the live wire is used by the current as an incoming passage. The black coloured wire is known as the neutral wire as used by the current as an exit passage from our homes. This passage completes the circuit and is a low resistance path for the current. The green coloured wire is known as the Earth wire is used as a passage for the flow of any leaked current and acts as a safety measure.
- The potential difference between the live and neutral wire is maintained at 220 V for domestic supply.
- When the live and neutral wire comes in contact then the current in the circuit promptly increases which causes fire. This is called short-circuiting.
- Using too many appliances from a single port/socket above its limit can lead to increase in the supply voltage. This problems is called Overloading.
- A fuse must be used in order to be protected from problems of overloading and short-circuiting.

CHAPTER AT A GLANCE – NCERT BASED IMPORTANT POINTS

- Magnetic field is the area around the magnet where its properties can be sensed.
- Magnetic field is represented by Magnetic field lines.
- In case of a straight current carrying conductor the field lines are in the shape of concentric circles.
- The magnetic field lines around a current carrying solenoid matches with the field lines around a bar magnet.
- When a current carrying conductor is placed in a magnetic field it experiences a force.

Question 1: Draw magnetic field lines around a bar magnet.

Answer 1:

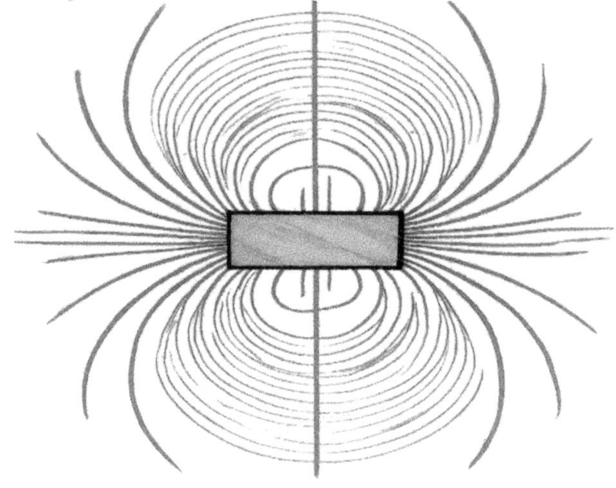

Question 2: List the properties of magnetic field lines.

Answer 2: Properties of magnetic field lines are:

◆ Outside a magnet the magnetic field lines emerge from the North pole and merge at the south pole.

◆ Inside a magnet the magnetic field lines move from South to North pole.

◆ The field lines are closed curves.

◆ The direction of field lines at a particular point on the line can be determined by making a tangent at that point.

◆ The degree of closeness of the lines determines the strength of the field.

◆ Two magnetic field lines never intersect each other. If we assume two lines to be intersecting at a point then it means that there would be two directions of the field at a point which is technically impossible.

Question 3: Why don't two magnetic field lines of force intersect each other?

Answer 3: Two magnetic field lines never intersect each other because if we assume two lines to be intersecting at a point then it means that there would be two directions of the field at a single point which is technically impossible.

Question 4: Consider a circular loop of wire lying in the plane of the table. Let the current pass through clockwise. Apply the right hand rule to find out the direction of the magnetic field inside and outside the loop.

Answer 4: The field lines inside the loop are moving into the table and those outside the loop are moving out of the table.

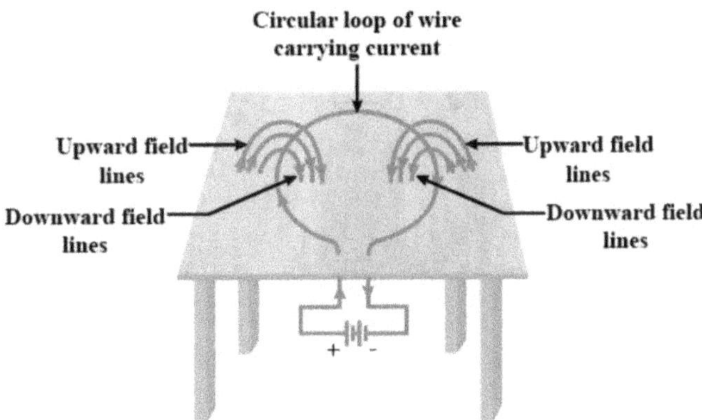

Question 5: The magnetic field in a given region is uniform. Draw a diagram to represent it.

Answer 5: Uniform magnetic field is represented by parallel line.

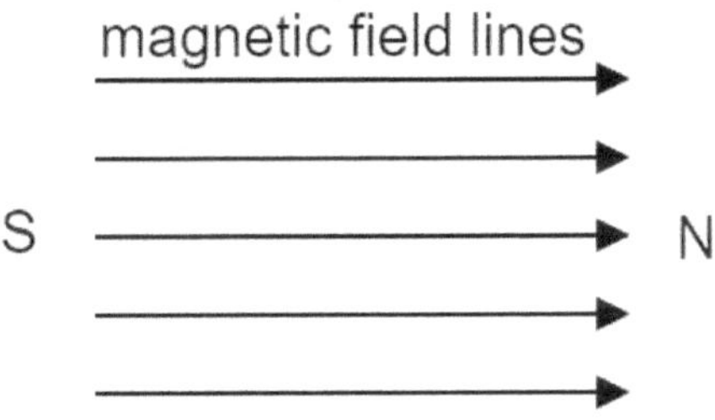

Question 6: Choose the correct option:
The magnetic field inside a long straight solenoid carrying current

a. is zero
b. decreases as we move towards its end.
c. increases as we move towards its end.
d. is the same at all points.

Answer 6: The correct option is;

d. is same at all points.

This is because the field strength inside a solenoid is uniform.

Question 7: Which of the following property if a proton can change while it moves freely in a magnetic field? (There may be more than one correct answers.)

a. mass

b. speed

c. velocity

d. momentum

Answer 7: If a proton moves freely in a magnetic field then its **velocity will change** due to change in its direction. Since its velocity changes so its **momentum will also change.**

Question 8: In activity 13.7, how do we think the displacement of rod AB will be affected if (i) current in the rod AB is increased; (ii) a stronger horse shoe magnet is used; and (iii) length of the rod AB is increased?

Answer 8:

(i) When the current in the rod is increased then it experience more force therefore the displacement will increase.

(ii) A strong horse shoe magnet will increase the amount of force and thus the displacement will increase.

(iii) Increase in the length of the rod will lead to increase in the amount of force experienced by the rod and thus the displacement of the rod will increase.

Question 9: A positively charged particle (alpha particle) projected towards west is deflected towards north by a magnetic field. The direction of the magnetic field is:

a. towards south   b. towards east   c. downward   d. upward

Answer 9: By using right hand thumb rule we get the direction of the magnetic field is **upward.**

Notes

Notes

Notes

Notes